Nomads of the Nomads

WORLDS
OF
MAN

Studies in
Cultural Ecology

EDITED BY

Walter Goldschmidt

University of California
Los Angeles

Nomads of the Nomads

The Āl Murrah Bedouin of the Empty Quarter

DONALD POWELL COLE

The American University in Cairo

Aldine Publishing Company / Chicago

Donald Powell Cole is Assistant Professor of Anthropology, The American University in Cairo. He received his M.A. and Ph.D. in Anthropology from the University of California at Berkeley, where he was Visiting Assistant Professor of Anthropology.

Frontispiece. The vegetation in the deserts of northeastern Arabia is much more varied and profuse than in the Rub' al-Khali. Because winter grasses quickly spring up after a rain, these areas are much prized by the Āl Murrah.

Cover. A boy sits on the top of a sand dune in the Rub' al-Khali.

First published 1975 by
Aldine Publishing Company
529 South Wabash Avenue
Chicago, Illinois 60605

ISBN 0–202–01117–8 clothbound edition
      0–202–01118–6 paperbound edition

Library of Congress Catalog Number 74–18211

Printed in the United States of America

To
Merzuq, Hurran,
and all the youth of the Āl Murrah
who face probably the greatest changes
of any people in the world.

Foreword

We are here in the presence of extremes: an area so desolate that it is known as the Empty Quarter—though it is by no means empty; a place inhabited by a people so purely and thoroughly devoted to their pastoral pursuits that they are referred to as the nomads of the nomads. To the urban and peasant Arabs nearby, it is a land inhabited by jinns, but to the Āl Murrah and other camel keeping pastoralists, it provides a rich and rewarding life, for the milk is the sweetest, the air is pure and all men are brothers.

For either to survive, men and camels must live in close symbiosis; each completely dependent upon the other. The camels provide food, fiber and transport; man provides the knowledge of available resources, of which the most precious are water and the grasses that grow where rains have fallen. Donald Cole shows us that this is more complex and intricate than such a simple statement would suggest.

First of all, there is the intricate knowledge of the desert itself—its varieties, its moods, its resources. So clever are these desert dwellers that they are thought to be the descendants of the spirits—the jinns—that inhabit this world. Next, there is the knowledge of the camels—their needs and capacities, and the peculiarities of each individual animal. Knowledge of the landscape and knowledge of the animals must be brought together so the scarce resources are fully utilized, yet carefully conserved.

To wrest their livelihood from this apparently inhospitable environment, men must work in collaboration, and as important as their technical knowledge—perhaps more important—is the structuring of social life. The tribesmen of the Empty Quarter must have a flexible social system, one that enables the individual household to operate alone when the environmental situation requires, and yet enables it to fit into a larger structure when the season demands. This means that it requires a pattern of independence and equality, while at the same time providing the necessary leadership. It means that each person must be capable of performing every necessary task, but that the chores be equitably shared by all.

The ecology of this camel pastoralism pervades every facet of Āl Murrah life, and much that has seemed mysterious becomes meaningful in this context. We see the relationships of men and women in terms of the close collaboration required between them, and discover the personal element in that most enigmatic aspect of their social organization—marriage *within* the lineage. We discover qualities of personality as these relate to the exigencies of desert existence, and we see how the religion of Islam is transformed by their special problems.

The Āl Murrah live according to ancient traditions forged in their desert environment, but this does not mean their life is unchanging. Cole shows us that already there are changes that began in 1932, when Saudi Arabia became a nation and intertribal raiding and warfare was brought to an end. He also shows the adaptability that they are bringing to bear as the desert is increasingly invaded by motor transport and oil rigs. Whether Āl Murrah life will survive in the Empty Quarter will depend on the wisdom of their national leadership in permitting them to make the necessary adjustments in their traditional system—adjustments that they are willing and able to make.

Man everywhere must attune his life to the requirements of his economy. In a place like the Arabian desert, which places severe limits on how one must live, these adjustments are most insistent. The tribes of the Empty Quarter show us that even when these demands pervade every facet of behavior, life can still be rich and rewarding.

Walter Goldschmidt

Contents

Photo section follows page 81

Contents

Preface

For two years, between April 1968 and May 1970, I had the good fortune to live in Saudi Arabia. I went there as a graduate student in anthropology to do research for my doctoral dissertation at the University of California, Berkeley. No academic anthropological research had every been carried out in Saudi Arabia and I went there as a kind of ethnographic explorer. At the suggestion of Dr. 'Abd al-Aziz al-Khuwaiter of the University of Riyadh and of Musa'ud al-Taji al-Faruki of the Saudi Arabian Ministry of Agriculture and Water, I decided to work among the Āl Murrah Bedouin tribe. The government of Saudi Arabia was developing a large-scale sedentarization project for nomads at Haradh and the Āl Murrah were being considered for inclusion in this project. Although I was skeptical about the merits of sedentarization projects, I welcomed this opportunity to work among one of the most traditional Bedouin tribes in Arabia and to make my research of some relevance to government administrators concerned about the development of their country.

I spent eighteen months with the Āl Murrah in the desert regions of eastern and southeastern Saudi Arabia. During most of this time, I lived as a permanent guest in the tent of 'Ali ibn Salem ibn al-Kurbi of the Āl 'Azab patrilineage. 'Ali's second oldest son, al-Kurbi, was hired as a driver-guide at my behest by the Saudi Arabian Ministry of Agriculture and Water, which also generously offered me the use of a pickup truck.

The realization of this study would have been impossible without the active cooperation and friendship of al-Kurbi who not only expertly guided me through the deserts of Saudi Arabia but guided me among the Āl Murrah as well. A young man in his early thirties, he welcomed me as a brother, helped me learn the Āl Murrah dialect of Arabic, and introduced me to hundreds of his fellow tribespeople. I also owe a special debt to his father, his father's brothers, and his mother's brothers for teaching me genealogies, for telling me stories about raids and the days of old, and for instructing me in the traditions of the Arab nomads. His brother, Merzuq, and his cousin, Hurran ibn Muhammad, both long-haired youths, taught me how to ride camels, took me herding with them, and taught me most of what I learned about the desert itself.

Because I lived with the Āl 'Azab patrilineage, those people are the ones I know best. But I also visited all the other lineages of the Āl Murrah and spent altogether about six weeks at different times with the amir of the Āl Murrah, Talib ibn Rashid ibn Shoraim, his son, Rashid, and his nephew, Faisal ibn Muhammad. All of the Āl Murrah received me with open hospitality and, in time, I became well known throughout the tribe and even among other tribes, for the news of the desert travels widely. They gave me the name of 'Abdallah and said that I was the son of the amir Talib. They said that I had come to Arabize myself, which was true in a way, and they took pleasure in teaching me the best etiquette and manners so that I could act as a *sharif*, or noble, tribesman. I spent the happiest months of my life with them and I can never fully repay them for all they taught me nor for the brotherly love they gave me.

Many others helped me in countless ways throughout my stay in Saudi Arabia. My deepest gratitude goes to His Majesty King Faisal ibn 'Abd al-Aziz Āl Faisal Āl Sa'ud, who personally approved my research program. For their continued support, encouragement, and hospitality I should like to especially acknowledge Princes Sa'ad ibn Faisal, 'Abdallah ibn 'Abd al-Aziz Āl Jiluwi, and Mansur ibn 'Abdallah ibn 'Abdurrahman; Shaikhs Ahmed Zaki al-Yamani and Hassan al-Mishari; Dr. 'Abd al-Aziz al-Kuwaiter; 'Abd al-Aziz al-Turki; Dr. Soraya M. al-Turki; Musa'ud al-Taji al-Faruki; Tarek al-Shawaf; Terry Timmons; and Vicki Caldwell Timmons. This study was financed by a research grant and fellowship from the U.S. National Institute of Mental Health, for which I am most appreciative.

This book is a completely revised version of my doctoral dissertation. My committee at Berkeley was composed of Professors Laura Nader, Nelson Graburn, and Mounah Khouri, all of whom helped me immensely in the preparation of that work. I should also like to thank Professors Robert Fernea and Talal Asad who read and commented in detail on my dissertation. The present presentation of the data and the interpretations expressed are, of course, my own responsibility.

There are always difficulties in transliterating Arabic into English. This is especially so when the speech of the group concerned varies widely from classical Arabic, as is the case with the Āl Murrah. I have tried to spell Arabic words as closely as possible to the way they are pronounced in the Āl Murrah colloquial dialect. Long and short vowels are not differentiated. An apostrophe, ', used for the glottal stop. The barred A in Āl is used to differentiate that word, meaning People, from the definite article in Arabic, al.

DONALD POWELL COLE

San Francisco
June 1974

THE ARABIAN PENINSULA

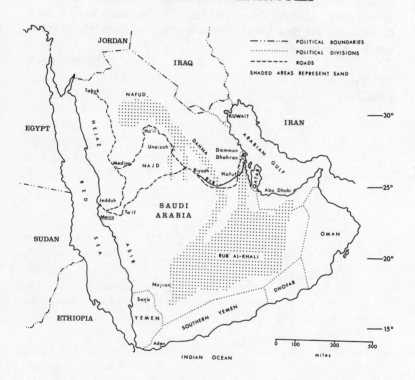

Figure 1

Chapter 1

INTRODUCTION

In late September 1968 after receiving permission from the government of the Kingdom of Saudi Arabia, I traveled to the headquarters of the amir of the Āl Murrah Bedouin tribe in an abandoned worker's barracks near the oil processing plant at Abquaiq, a town in eastern Saudi Arabia. The amir, Talib ibn Rashid ibn Shoraim al-Marri, doubles as paramount chief of the Āl Murrah and as head of a unit of the Saudi Arabian Reserve National Guard of which most of the members are from the Āl Murrah tribe.

I was hospitably welcomed by the amir, his sons, and his father's brother's sons and during the following days introduced to scores of tribesmen who had come to perform their monthly duties in the National Guard and to collect their salaries. The amir and his eldest son, Rashid, took pains to teach me the genealogy of the Āl Murrah and to tell me something of their history. Most of the other men spontaneously told me the names of the *fakhds,* or lineages, from which they came, as well as the names of other kinship groupings, all of which they would ask me to repeat. I was exhilarated by the open, straightforward, friendly manner in which these men presented themselves. They always seemed to be laughing and playing jokes on each other and on me.

Their friendly gregariousness was in contrast to descriptions I had read and heard of Saudi Arabian Bedouin as dour fanatics who, with their long hair and daggers, are barbarians who appreciate few of the finer things of life. It also contrasted with descriptions of the desert region the Āl Murrah inhabit, the Rub' al-Khali (the Empty Quarter), as a barren land of madness and death. These Āl Murrah always said, "In the Rub' al-Khali you will find everything: the best camels, plenty of good camel's milk, lots of hunting, clean sand and fresh air, and only one's brothers—everything." Throughout the eighteen months I lived with them, I never thought of them as barbaric or fanatical. Rather, a feeling of what I would call aristocratic simplicity was continuously confirmed by their actions and their talk. They reject the city as physically and socially polluted and prefer the desert where they can live what they habitually describe as a pure and clean life. Their rejection of the security of sedentary life is coupled with an adherence to an austere practice of Islam as taught by the strict Handbali Sunnites and a high valuation of the ways of the Arabs—of being generous and dispensing hospitality, of seeking revenge when wronged, and of marrying only people of one's kind.

But these people, content to keep to themselves and to exploit an ecological niche that has provided them with a relatively high level of subsistence within traditional Arabia, are now being faced with what may well be a life or death struggle for survival. What is in question does not concern so much the physical life of individual beings but whether their society, their culture, and their way of life, have a place—even in some modified form—in modern Saudi Arabia.

The world's richest known oil fields lie in eastern Saudi Arabia and its brother states that bound the Arabian Gulf. Oil was discovered in Saudi Arabia in 1938; its most rapid exploitation began after World War II; revenues rose from $5 million in 1950 to nearly $1 billion in 1968 and to over $3 billion in 1973. Into this area, the cradle of the desert Arabs and of Islam itself, have gushed the consumer products of both Western and Eastern industrial economies. Trucks, cars, and airplanes have replaced camels, which had been the only means of transportation within the lifetime of people no older than thirty. Within the past ten years, the old labyrinthine mud-brick cities have felt the tread of the bulldozer opening up broad, straight thoroughfares and are crumbling as the old houses are abandoned for modern air-conditioned villas in the suburbs or high-rise apartment buildings.

The cities have changed tremendously and are today booming with new schools and universities, with hospitals, with commercial establishments selling products from most of the industrial world, and with paved streets and broad avenues that extend for miles around the sprawling cities of Riyadh and Jeddah. To the cities and oil camps has also come a large migration of Lebanese, Palestinian, and Egyptian middle-class people, of workers from the poorer and more traditional areas of the Yemen, Hadhramaut, and Oman, and of European, North American, Pakistani, and Japanese advisers, technicians, skilled laborers, and company managers.

The towns and cities have changed more than the villages or the desert but the delicate balance between the desert and the sown, between nomadic pastoralist and sedentary farmer, has been destroyed. The majority of the nomads, probably twenty per cent of an estimated total population of eight million, continue to herd animals in the desert and to provide for their basic subsistence, but more and more of their youth are leaving the tents and the herds to seek jobs as wage laborers in the cities and oil camps. Many are staying on, bringing their wives and children, and settling down to a life as members of a wage-earning proletariat rather than as independent tribespeople.

The future of nomadism is thus uncertain. Certainly they are already changing, but is nomadic pastoralism itself altogether doomed in contemporary Saudi Arabia? Why is it cheaper and easier to import frozen mutton from Argentina and New Zealand than to use national products? Do not the deserts of Arabia still bloom and provide the grazing lands that used to allow the export of large numbers of camels, sheep, and goats throughout the Levant and to Egypt and India? Cannot the exploitation of these lands be made to contribute to the rapidly developing cash-oriented economy? These are questions we seek to answer in the latter part of this book, but they should be kept in the back of the reader's mind throughout, for they form part of the reality nomads face in today's Arabia.

Before attempting to analyze the changes faced by nomads in Saudi Arabia, and indeed in much of the rest of the Arab world, let us turn first to a discussion of nomadic pastoralism in Arabia in its more traditional aspects. The Bedouin of Arabia have always represented only part of the total population of the area. Despite the myths of many of the sedentary people who claim to have descended from nomads, most desert people have probably always been villagers living in oases. The nomads, however, are the ones who capture the attention of travelers and who have provided much of the ethos of traditional Arabia as a whole.

In this book, we turn our attention to the nomads not because they represented an idealized and romanticized version of the "true Arab," but because we are interested in seeing how they manage to live in an environment that most people regard as more than merely inhospitable—as a land of madness and death incapable of supporting human life. They are highly skilled specialists enjoying a relatively comfortable life in a harsh environment. How do they do it?

The perspective we take is ecological. How is the social structure and culture of the Bedouins adapted to their life as nomadic pastoralists? Especially, what kinds of social groups exist within their society and how do these provide an organizational framework for the exploitation of their environment? How is the process of fission and fusion of social units, of contracting and expanding, that is so much a part of the dynamics of Bedouin social organization related to seasonal changes and to the needs of their animals? How does their desert habitation and their intimate association with animals affect their religious and symbolic life? And how are all these aspects of their life interrelated to form a coherent whole that until recently has been transmitted from generation to generation almost without change?

NOMADIC PASTORALISM IN THE MIDDLE EAST

The primarily Islamic lands of Southwest Asia and North Africa, commonly referred to as the Middle East, display a number of physical characteristics that favor the combination of sedentary agriculture and nomadic pastoralism. Rainfall is generally low and almost nowhere reaches the 40- to 50-inch yearly levels that are characteristic of the eastern United States, western Europe, sub-Saharan Africa, India, and China. Only a few coastal and mountain areas receive as much as 20 inches per year, which is equal to the drier parts of Spain. Rainfall in the rest of the area varies from less than 1 inch per year in the central Sahara Desert and southern Egypt to 4 inches in the deserts of southern Arabia and to as much as 8 inches in northern Arabia and the Syrian Desert.

Although agriculture is severely limited to less than 10 percent of the total land mass because of lack of water, some of the world's most famous agrarian states and empires have been located in this area. Most of the crops and animals that we in the West know and use today were first domesticated here during the early period of the Agricultural Revolution, at least 10,000 years ago. Agriculture, of course, has been highly concentrated in a few areas that can be irrigated. The valleys of the famous river systems of the Middle East, most notably the Tigris-Euphrates and the Nile, have known large scale irrigation projects since at least 7,500 B.P. and are associated not only with highly intensive agriculture but with the development of urban living and the division of society into a number of different economic specializations. The state, as an institution, also had its earliest development in these agricultural centers of the Middle East.

The emergence of pastoralism as a specialized form of activity dates from the same period as the emergence of agriculture in the Middle East. Archaeological evidence presents us with a picture of agriculture and pastoralism developing more or less concomitantly and in close symbiotic relationship. Equally early dates are found for both animal and plant domesticants, which suggests a general regionwide process of cultural and ecological change. Over 10,000 years ago when hunter-gatherers first began the process of selective harvesting and of seed planting that led to increased yields and the onset of sedentary village life, they also began to control the movements of herds of wild sheep and goats to keep them permanently on the margins of grain fields. Some of these animals were captured, penned, and domesticated. As agriculture continued to develop and population densities increased, more economic specializations emerged. Eventually, full-time herders appeared, especially as they began to exploit pasture areas further removed from the centers of cultivation.

Nomadic pastoralism is thus not a holdover of the hunter-gatherer way of life of our paleolithic ancestors. Unlike the wild animals on which hunter-gatherers depend and over which they have little, if any, control, the domesticated animals of pastoralists have been brought under their cultural control and are dependent on their human herders for survival. Nomadic pastoralism represents an attempt on the part of Middle Eastern peoples to utilize areas that are not conducive to agriculture but which provide the potential for high returns through the rational pasturing of animals by skilled herders.

Although agriculture is limited to less than 10 percent of the area, the rest of the land mass is by no means totally devoid of plant life. Indeed, excellent natural pasture areas abound with a large variety of perennial and annual plants. But seldom do climatic conditions provide the potential for sedentary pastoralism as in modern ranching. Pasture areas are limited and the only means of exploiting them is through seasonal migrations from one to another.

In some areas of the Middle East, the juxtaposition of two ecological zones that are complementary to each other on a seasonal basis encourages nomadic pastoralism. In western and southwestern Iran, for example, the Zagros Mountains annually receive large quantities of winter snow and rain that provide the basis for natural summer pastures. Just to the west of the Zagros lies the Assyrian steppe, which has good winter pastures but is hot and dry in summer. In prehistoric times, hunters followed wild animals in seasonal migrations between these two areas; now herders drive their animals from winter pastures on the Assyrian steppe to summer ones in the valleys of the Zagros. A similar situation occurs in Morocco where pastoralists graze their animals on the steppe lands on the northern edge of the Sahara Desert in winter and then move up to pastures in the valleys of the Atlas Mountains in summer.

In these areas and in other places where such a juxtaposition of lowland and highland pastures occurs, nomadic pastoralists interact with sedentary agriculturalists with whom they maintain strong social, economic, and cultural ties. Each group specializes in exploiting only one part of the total environment. In the Zagros since ancient times, pastoralists have used the higher and drier valleys that are not conducive to agriculture while farmers have exploited the broader valleys that receive more annual rainfall. Similarly, on the Assyrian steppe the pastoralists use those areas that are too salty to support agriculture while the richer areas are farmed.

The conditions that underlie nomadic pastoralism in the vast deserts of the Middle East are different. Seasonal migrations occur, but instead of moving vertically from lowland winter to highland summer pastures, the pattern of movement is horizontal, from permanent sources of water in summer to fall, winter, and spring pastures. The crucial factor under these conditions is not the availability of complementary zones but the need of certain animals to drink regularly and often only during the hot summers but not during the cooler seasons. Such, of course, are the characteristics of that specially adapted animal, the camel. The ability of camels to survive without drinking for long periods is not due so much to their proverbial ability to store up large quantities of water as to their "cooling system," which allows them to withstand high degrees of heat with a minimum expenditure of liquids. In the deserts of Arabia, camels drink once every four days during the summer, about once every week or ten days during the fall and spring, and sometimes only once a month or every six weeks during the winter, depending on the temperature and the availability of fresh winter grasses rich in moisture. Some varieties of sheep and goat have a similar ability to forego water, but not to the same extent as camels.

Not everywhere does nomadic pastoralism represent the optimal pattern of land use, now or in earlier years. Throughout North Africa, for example, Arab nomads during the eleventh century A.D. destroyed much of the irrigation works established by the Romans and maintained by the urban Arabs following the Islamic conquests in the seventh century. The well-watered Atlantic coast of Morocco and the Mediterranean coast of Morocco, Algeria, and Tunisia were occupied during the nomadic invasions by Arab tribes who concentrated mainly on pastoralism rather than continuing the highly productive agricultural activities of the former occupants. Only in this century has much of this land been returned to agriculture. At other periods of history, nomadic pastoralists have similarly interfered with agriculture. During the seventeenth and eighteenth centuries, nomadic tribes gained considerable *de facto* power throughout Syria, where they consistently threatened trade and commerce as well as agriculture by demanding special payments for "protection." Indeed, one scholar (Issawi 1969:105) attributes the rise in urban population during this period mainly to the upheaval and instability wreaked in rural areas by nomadic pastoralists.

Since the end of the eighteenth century, however, nomads throughout the area have consistently been declining in importance relative to the sedentary population. Political as well as economic factors, both internal and external, have caused a decline of nomadic pastoralism and in the importance of tribes in the socio-political structure. This process of change has been both subtle and violent but always complex. In many instances—in Morocco, Algeria, Tunisia, Libya, and Palestine—it has been much complicated by settler colonialism. Those areas that escaped large-scale European settlement have nonetheless suffered from the meddling of European imperialists in internal tribal affairs which they seldom understood.

In recent decades, the discovery of oil and the vast riches it has created seem to have sounded the death knell for nomadic pastoralism as an important way of life in any significant part of the Middle East. The contemporary ideology of the governments and of the urban masses is strongly against the continuation of nomadism, which is regarded as contrary to the goals and aspirations of a modern nation and society.

Although large-scale industrialization must eventually result in basic alterations in the subsistence-oriented economies of both nomadic pastoralists and sedentary farmers, we should be cautious in juxtaposing these two sectors. They do have contrastingly different life styles and have often been in conflict over political control of much of the Middle East, but an overall ecological perspective of the region shows a gradation of specializations that reflects attempts to exploit the total environment and to leave no part of it unused.

While the physical boundary between the desert and the sown is strikingly sharp in the Middle East—one can often stand with one foot in a rich agricultural land and the other in the desert—the boundary between nomadic pastoralist and sedentary farmer is less precise. Except in those areas that receive adequate rainfall, the limit of agriculture is directly tied to how far irrigation water can be extended into the desert. Different types of pastoralism and different degrees of nomadism occur, depending on whether the pastoralists operate mainly close to agricultural centers or deep within the desert. Some pastoralists operate on the edge of the desert and play important roles in the agricultural sector. Many of these are associated with the herding of sheep and goats. Others operate deep within the desert, far from agricultural centers, and seldom interact with agriculturalists. Most of these are traditionally associated with the herding of camels. There is thus a continuum that runs the gamut from sedentary agriculturalists through transhumant agriculturalists, semisedentary pastoralists, and pastoralists who also engage in some agriculture to full-time nomadic pastoralists. Nonpastoral nomads, such as gypsies, also contribute to the variety of peoples in the Middle East.

Intricately complex patterns of economic interaction exist between the sedentary and nomadic populations. Nomads pasture their animals on the stubble of the fields after harvest and in the process contribute manure to the fields. Many of the nomads who operate near agricultural centers play important roles in transporting crops, since they own the major beast of burden in the Middle East, the camel. Many sedentary people own animals which they entrust to nomads who graze them on the rich desert grasses and shrubs. Similarly, nomads often own palm trees or agricultural plots which they entrust to the care of agricultural specialists in return for a part of the harvest. The warrior nomads who most often frequent the innermost reaches of the desert guarantee the protection of both sedentary farmer and semisedentary pastoralist against attack or exploitation by other nomads. Thus both groups, nomads and sedentaries, depend on the products and services of each other. Although each group likes to think of itself apart and contrasts its way of life with that of the other group, all are organized in a single economic system geared to the utilization of all the resources, agricultural and pastoral, of the total environment. Consequently, any attempts at modernization which lead to the sedentarization of the nomads must result in the loss of what has been a highly productive part of the total resources of the Middle East.

THE ĀL MURRAH

The Āl Murrah, who are the subject of this book, are an Arab (or Bedouin) tribe who exploit the deserts of the southeastern and eastern parts of the Arabian Peninsula. Although no census has been made of them, they probably number about 15,000 people. They divide themselves into a number of different patrilineal descent groups. The most basic unit of their society is the patrilocal household composed of an old man and old woman, their sons and their sons' wives, and their children. Households average about seven people. Above the level of the household is the lineage which includes all the people descended from a male ancestor who lived about five generations ago; a lineage averages about fifty households. From four to six lineages unite, according to the patterns of patrilineal descent, to form clans. The Āl Murrah tribe, which includes all the descendants of Murrah, is composed of seven clans.

The Āl Murrah stand at the extreme end of the nomad-sedentary spectrum and are highly mobile camel nomads. Although a few of them are now following precedents set by other Arabian tribes and are switching to market-oriented sheep and goat herding and are seeking wage labor, the vast majority of the tribe still depends on subsistence-oriented camel herding in which camels are raised primarily for milk. They are among the most traditional nomads in contemporary Saudi Arabia, but they are well aware of the important changes now occurring.

Unlike romantic Westerners who bemoan the passing of this ancient way of life and fear that debasement and moral bankruptcy will replace the proud, aristocratic ways of the desert Arabs, the Āl Murrah praise Allah for the security and peace that today characterize most tribal affairs in Arabia and for the easier life that modern economic development is making possible. Furthermore, they do not agree with either the Westerners or the governmental officials that nomadic pastoralism is doomed in the modern world. Rather, they are seeking ways—with little outside help or encouragement—to modernize their pastoralism and to become more actively involved in modern society. That the Āl Murrah themselves have not changed as much as other tribes is due to their occupation of the most remote and isolated desert region of Arabia, the Rub' al-Khali, and, as they say, to their love for the fine herds of purebred camels which they cannot imagine abandoning.

Although much of their domain lies in the most isolated part of Arabia, most of Saudi Arabia's oil is located within parts of their territories or very near them. As a result, the Āl Murrah have observed even more radical changes than most other tribes, which occupy regions further removed from the sites of the oil industry. They offer a unique perspective on the traditional patterns of pastoral nomadism in the deserts of Arabia and, at the same time, a glimpse of the major factors of change that operate there and throughout much of the Middle East today.

Chapter 2

THE ENVIRONMENT: LAND, ANIMALS, AND SPECIAL SKILLS

The Āl Murrah provide for most, though not all, of their subsistence through the herding of camels, sheep, and goats in the deserts of eastern and southeastern Arabia. Camels are the most important species of animals to the Āl Murrah and were the only animals kept by the Āl 'Azab lineage among whom I lived and traveled. Like all pastoral peoples, the Āl Murrah have a close symbiotic relationship with the animals they herd. These animals provide them with the staples of their diet, and the Āl Murrah work hard to search out the best pastures and to obtain and keep control of sure sources of water. As animal species, both the humans and the camels are necessary for each other's survival. Neither species could live alone in the desert environment they inhabit without the contributions of the other.

The close relationship pastoralists maintain with the animals they herd and live off is one of the most striking features of pastoral societies. The animals not only contribute to sustaining their material existence but they figure prominently in the folklore and religion of the people. The Āl Murrah not only drink the milk of their camels but they give them names, make up poems and songs about them, and tell endless stories about them. They have special ways of talking to them and they say they are able to communicate with them. They are such an integral part of every aspect of their lives—physical, social, and cultural—that it is hard to conceive of the Āl Murrah without their camels. The camels are their abiding passion.

The most prominent element in the diet of the Āl Murrah is milk. The camels they herd are special breeds famous for their milk. After the birth of a calf, a she-camel provides at least a gallon of milk daily for human consumption and continues to produce milk, though in slightly reduced quantity, for at least a year. Camels also provide an occasional source of meat, although the Āl Murrah rarely slaughter a full-grown camel unless it is obviously sick and about to die. They occasionally slaughter newborn calves, but they do not rely on their camels for regular sources of protein. Before most of the game was killed off during the last few decades, hunting wild animals provided a more regular source of animal protein. Nowadays, sheep, purchased in urban markets or from other Bedouins, are the major source of meat; but meat is not a regular part of their diet. Milk is the basic element, and they continuously talk about how good it is and how it gives strength and power. When they must travel away from their herds, for example to the cities, they always yearn for the sweet milk of their beloved camels.

The other staple of their diet is dates. Meals of rice or bread, with animal fat poured over it, are also consumed almost daily. The Āl Murrah obtain all but a small portion of the dates they consume through cash purchases in urban markets, especially in Hofuf. The money for these purchases comes from their activities in the Reserve National Guard of Saudi Arabia and, increasingly, from wages for labor in the cities and oil camps of eastern Arabia. They almost never sell any of their camels and do not depend on them or their products for securing the other elements in their diet. They do depend, however, on prestations, or special payments, from the government. In the old days, before the development of a strong central government and the incorporation of the tribes into the National Guard and before the development of a cash economy, the Bedouins had special relationships with urban centers and villages: they would receive annual payments of dates and grains in return for their guaranteed protection of urban markets and peasant fields from disruption or plunder by other tribes. Now they receive cash from the National Guard and use it to purchase most of their necessities. In later chapters, we will discuss in greater detail the relationship of the Bedouins with the wider society in which they live. But the heart and mind of the Āl Murrah is with their animals deep inside the desert. In this chapter, let us look at the physical characteristics of the land they inhabit, at the herds they keep, at the rhythm of their migrations, and at the skills and specialized knowledge they have developed in their age-old struggle for survival with freedom and dignity.

ĀL MURRAH TERRITORIES

Since before they can remember, the Āl Murrah have exploited a vast area of southeastern and eastern Arabia that includes a core area, known as *dirat-Āl Murrah,* Āl Murrah territories, and several outlying areas that are shared with other tribes during winter and spring pastures. *Dirat-Āl Murrah,* almost all of which is located within the national boundaries of the contemporary Kingdom of Saudi Arabia, covers approximately 250,000 square miles and is by far the largest and least densely populated territory of any Arabian tribe. No formalized demarcations of either national or tribal origin separate this area, taken as a whole, from that of other tribes, or internally among the various subdivisions of the Āl Murrah. The area of the Āl Murrah does, however, contain within itself certain geographic boundaries and is exploited according to natural geographic subdivisions.

They claim Najran, an oasis near the southwest corner of the Rub' al-Khali, as their place of origin, although the majority of the tribe at present does not include Najran within its normal field of action. Their territories extend from Najran northeastward in an arc across the western and central areas of the Rub' al-Khali, the southern edge of which marks their own southernmost boundary. From the eastern pa.t of the Rub' al-Khali they extend northward, including the Dahna sand dunes and mountains on the west and the Jafurah sand desert on the east. The traditional northern boundary of Āl Murrah territories is the area around the oasis of al-Hasa, although during winter and spring pastures they range as far north as Kuwait and southern Iraq. Their own traditional wells, to which they claim exclusive rights, are located from immediately south of al-Hasa all the way into the central

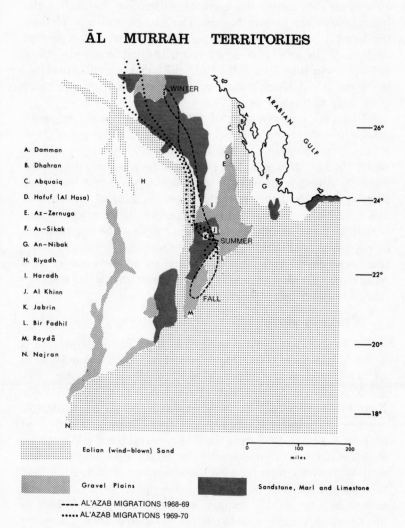

ĀL MURRAH TERRITORIES

A. Damman

B. Dhahran

C. Abquaiq

D. Hofuf (Al Hasa)

E. Az-Zernuga

F. As-Sikak

G. An-Nibak

H. Riyadh

I. Haradh

J. Al Khinn

K. Jabrin

L. Bir Fadhil

M. Raydā

N. Najran

WINTER

ARABIAN GULF

SUMMER

FALL

—26°

—24°

—22°

—20°

—18°

Eolian (wind-blown) Sand

Gravel Plains

Sandstone, Marl and Limestone

0   100   200
miles

- - - - AL'AZAB MIGRATIONS 1968-69

• • • • AL'AZAB MIGRATIONS 1969-70

Figure 2

sands of the Rub' al-Khali, with another set of wells in the Najran area.

The Āl Murrah come regularly into contact with other tribes only when they are to the north of al-Hasa, to the east of the Jafurah or in the area of Najran. The vast central core of their territories is almost never frequented by other tribes except occasionally by small parties of a few tribes that have wells either within or near the edges of the Rub' al-Khali. Generally speaking, however, the Āl Murrah have an area about as large as France exclusively to themselves.

Within the northern part of this area they have four small oases where they grow date palms. The oldest and largest of these is Jabrin, with al-Khinn, as-Sikak, and an-Nibak having developed within the last fifty years. The oases are occupied only during the summer, although all of them have some permanent buildings. Primary schools have recently been established at all but al-Khinn. No more than a third of the tribe has any connection with these oases, and the rest summer at wells without agriculture or any permanent buildings. In this respect, the Āl Murrah differ from most Saudi Arabian nomads who spend the summer near small oases that have communities of permanently settled peasants related to the tribe.

The Rub' al-Khali

To outsiders, what is most striking about the Āl Murrah is their inhabitation of the vast and mysterious region of southeastern Arabia known as the Rub' al-Khali, the Empty Quarter. This 200,000-square mile area, one of the last regions to experience European exploration, has only gradually begun to divulge its mysteries to curious Westerners. Bertram Thomas in 1931 and St. John Philby in 1932 were the first to travel there and to prove that it was known to and used by at least some Bedouin tribesmen. Wilfred Thesiger traveled there more extensively from 1945 to 1950 and has left us a moving description of the wild and savage beauty of this solitary and demanding land, and of his traveling companions from the Āl Rashid tribe (Thesiger 1959). More recently, oil workers and geological survey teams have criss-crossed most of the area on land and in the air and have provided excellent maps.

All these travelers have experienced the Rub' al-Khali as a wild and harsh land where the edge of survival is very thin. None have known its more benign and pleasant aspects, for none have lived there with an indigenous community in the course of its normal activities. All have used Bedouin guides, but they have traveled separately from the herds and the herders. To go there without the herds is, as the Āl Murrah say, to court death. With the herds, it can be a land of plenty.

Most sedentary Saudi Arabians, as well as most foreigners, take its name literally and assume that the Empty Quarter is uninhabited. Both Dickson (1949:287) and Thesiger (1959:37) assert that the term *ar-rub' al-khali* was unfamiliar to the Bedouins they knew, and they assume that its use reflects the sedentary peoples' general ignorance of desert life and their fear of this marginal area as inhabited only by *jinns*, spirits, and devils. The Āl Murrah, however, habitually use it as a general term for the entire area, which they further break down into a number of named geographic subdivisions. That all these smaller areas are together referred to as the Rub' al-Khali is—according to the Āl Murrah—because of the absence of permanent settlements within its confines. It does not mean that nomads do not regularly exploit it and depend on it for much of their basic subsistence.

The Rub' al-Khali is separated from the more populated areas of the northeastern Arabia by wide gravel plains that are devoid of vegetation. These begin about thirty miles south of Jabrin, the small date palm oasis of the Āl Murrah that is the last agricultural settlement before the Rub' al-Khali. These plains extend for at least 350 miles across the central face of the Rub' al-Khali and for as much as 50 miles across. From the west, they run from the southern end of the Dahna, a narrow strip of sand dunes and sand mountains that is itself a major geographical boundary between the peoples of eastern and central Arabia. The Dahna runs in an arc from the Great Nafud sand desert of northwestern Arabia and ends in the southwestern edge of the Rub' al-Khali. The nomadic movements of eastern Arabian tribes are in north-south directions and seldom cross its western edge, although tribes from the southwest sometimes cross it into northeastern Arabia.

Once across the gravel plains, the Āl Murrah are in the land they say has everything: clean sand, fresh air, the best plants for camels, good hunting, and only one's brothers. Not all the Āl Murrah regularly utilize this area but all their really fine herds of milk camels, probably the best in all Arabia, are based here. Their owners and herders, about one-third of the tribe, are known proudly as *bedu al-bedu,* nomads of the nomads. The group I lived with, from the Āl 'Azab lineage of the Āl Murrah, are such, and it is they I describe in most detail in this book.

Vegetation in the Rub' al-Khali, and hence its potential for pastoral exploitation, is associated directly with sand. One estimate is that the Rub' al-Khali contains as much as 4,000 cubic miles of sand (Cressey 1960:83). The Āl Murrah recognize three major types of sand formation, the *jazirah* (island), the *goz* (sand hill) and the *'erg* (sand dune). The *jazirahs* are small patches of sand that appear scattered across the barren gravel plains and support a few desert grasses. They are no more than a few inches higher than the plain. The *goz* are gently rolling sand hills that reach thirty to forty feet above the floor of the plain and support both bushes and grass.

The *'erg* is the third and most spectacular feature of the Rub' al-Khali. In its central and western parts, dunes vary between twenty-five and one hundred miles in length and from several hundred yards to two miles in width. They are parallel to each other, running always in a southwest-northeast direction. The sharp crests of the dunes reach a height of 100 to 200 feet. Bushes and various types of desert grasses grow at the foot of the *'erg* and in sandy areas that sometimes stretch for miles behind them. The most important single plant here and in the *goz* is a bush called *abal.* According to the Āl Murrah, this bush stays green for at least four years after a single rain and maintains its moisture for several seasons.

To the north of the Rub' al-Khali, Āl Murrah territories include two contiguous strips of land which run in a north-south direction. The geology and flora is different in each but the two strips are not used complementarily. One is a continuation of the sands of the Rub' al-Khali and is known as the Jafurah Desert. It lies across the base of the Qatar Peninsula and runs north to the area of al-Hasa. The sand surfaces here are rolling, with dunes and steep slopes being uncommon.

The other strip lies to the west of the Jafurah from which it is separated by extensive gravel plains. It comprises approximately the southern half of an area known as the Summan. It is an area of sandy limestone dotted with hills and small mountains that has seen considerable erosion. Vegetation is sparse except in *wadis,* underground water courses that cross the area in an east-west direction. Some of these are great and impressive valleys, sometimes ten miles across, while others are narrow strips of no more than fifty feet across. Vegetation in the wadis is permanent owing to the underground water, and since these areas also tend to be sandy, grasses sprout up quickly after any good shower.

The other areas which the Āl Murrah exploit do not fall within what is strictly speaking *dirat-Āl Murrah,* but they are contiguous to the core area. They include the area from al-Hasa as far north as southern Iraq and Kuwait, the Qatar Peninsula, and the areas bordering the Rub' al-Khali in the extreme southwest. The utilization of these areas takes place during the winter and spring and is determined by the state of the pasturage in each, which in turn reflects the pattern of rainfall during any given year and the presence of other nomads.

WATER

Nomadic pastoralism in the Arabian Peninsula is determined by the pattern of rainfall and is dependent on access to underground sources of water. Until the drilling of modern government-owned wells, access to underground sources of water was almost exclusively determined by kin-based patterns of ownership, mitigated only by short-term hospitality. Access to pastures blessed by rainfall is, however, a more open matter in which the rights of first-come, first-served prevail, at least within broad limits.

With regard to rainfall, the Rub' al-Khali lies in a no man's land between two climatic zones. The southern coastal area of the Arabian Peninsula and the highland areas of the Yemen, the Asir, and the southern Hejaz are regularly watered each year by summer monsoon rains that come from the Indian Ocean. None of these reach the central areas of the Rub' al-Khali, but some occasionally spill over into its southern, western, and extreme eastern edges. The other climatic zone is that of most of the Middle East, in which northerly winds prevail, with dry summers and variable winters.

Northern Arabia is watered by winter rains which usually accompany cold fronts from the north. Occasionally these rains are general across the whole of northern Arabia but usually they are spotty. They tend to come in waves, beginning sometimes as early as November and continuing more or less through March. Localized thundershowers sometimes occur during the spring and as late as mid-June. The nomads classify the winter rains according to when they fall, since winter grasses appear in relation to when the rain fell. Reporting on the location and amount of each rain is a major topic of discussion, at least during the fall and winter, since the rain is the major determinant of migrations.

The northern part of the Rub' al-Khali is watered by winter rains, but these rarely reach the area until late in the season and are fewer in number than the rains that fall more to the north. Nevertheless, this displacement in time means that the southern pasture areas are likely to be fresh when the Āl Murrah return in late spring from winter pastures in the north.

There are years, of course, in which little or no rainfall accompanies the cold winter northers, causing drought in Saudi Arabia. Until a year before my arrival in 1968, there had been a prolonged drought of about ten years, and many herds of sheep, goats, and camels had died. In such years, some of the Āl Murrah take advantage of their ties with the territory around Najran in the southwest and take their herds across the Rub' al-Khali to graze in the monsoon-watered pasture lands there.

In 1967-68, excellent rains fell throughout the north, and the Āl Murrah named this year *az-ziman al-aishb,* the season of winter grasses. Good rains also fell during the winters of 1968-69 and 1969-70, although in the latter year they were more scattered. The southern Summan, the Jafurah, and the north central Rub' al-Khali received two good late spring rains in 1969. As a result, all of these areas were exceptionally rich in pasturage, for which unusual bounty the Āl Murrah never ceased to praise Allah. In 1968-69, we had no news of any rains in the central Rub' al-Khali, and only a very light shower fell near Rayda in the west. In the late winter of 1970, light showers fell in and around Jabrin, with good rains reported for the northeast and east central areas of the Rub' al-Khali. Again, no rain fell in the area around Rayda but we had enthusiastic reports of big rains in the western third of the Rub' al-Khali. In 1970, the north central pasture areas around Bir Fadhil were still in excellent condition after the two rains they had received in the spring of 1969. These areas, however, had hardly been touched in the previous seasons, since the nomads preferred to exploit the less enduring vegetation around Jabrin and to save the Rub' al-Khali for possible use in the next year.

Wilfred Thesiger characterized the climate of the Rub' al-Khali in the following terms:

A cloud gathers, the rain falls, men live; the cloud disperses without rain, and men and animals die. In the deserts of southern Arabia there is no rhythm of the seasons, no rise and fall of sap, but empty wastes where only the changing temperature marks the passage of the year. It is a bitter, dessicated land which knows nothing of gentleness or ease. [Thesiger 1959:1]

Such is hardly the situation as experienced by the Āl Murrah. They are not tied to exploiting a single area throughout the year, and if "the cloud disperses without rain," they take their animals to a place where rain has fallen. Thesiger himself was the first Westerner to show that rain almost always falls somewhere in the Rub' al-Khali every year. And since one rain of a few hours duration is enough to sustain the major vegetation for at least four years, the chances are very good for the continuous existence of some kind of pasture throughout the area. This is even more true if none of the area is overgrazed, a hazard the Āl Murrah avoid by keeping their camels continuously on the move, even during the hot summer months. They consciously keep the Rub' al-Khali as a kind of preserve and move out of this ecological zone at every possible chance to take advantage of the shorter-lived grasses of more benign zones.

Another key feature in the pastoral exploitation of desert Arabia is the existence and maintenance of wells. The Āl Murrah have a series of about twenty major wells scattered across the east central part of the Rub' al-Khali at distances varying between fifty and one hundred miles. They have at least an equal number of wells in their other territories to the north. Three major types of wells are distinguished by them. These include the *bir*, a deep, open-faced well out of which water is drawn in leather buckets, usually with the use of camel power; the *galamat*, a small-bore shaft out of which water flows freely; and the *'ain*, which is either a deep modern well with a mechanical pump or a large open well in which water, spring-like, comes naturally near the surface. None of the major Āl Murrah wells were dug by them. They say, "Our ancestors had them, but they are from the time of the Jahiliya, the Days of Ignorance" (i.e., before Islam).

HERDS

The Āl Murrah, and especially the Āl 'Azab on whom this book is focused, base their subsistence on camels. No sheep or goats are kept by any of the Āl Murrah who frequent the Rub' al-Khali, and never do any households in the tribe mix camels with sheep and goats. In this respect, they differ from other nomadic pastoralists, such as the Kababish Arabs of the Sudan.

Camels are capable of longer and faster moves than are sheep and goats and have a greater capacity for grazing pastures far distant from sources of water, as well as from home base. Mixed herds require a division of the herding units, at least during certain seasons. The Kababish obtain this at considerable expense to the individual household, which has to split up during the dry season as some members follow the camels and others stay with the sheep and goats. The Āl Murrah achieve this division of labor between households, so that if a sheep and goat herding household owns some camels (as is usual now, for a growing group of the Āl Murrah are switching to sheep and goats from camels), they entrust them to the care of a related household that specializes in herding camels.

There are many types of camels. Some are specialized as beasts of burden and are strong but slow and rough in their gait. Others, mainly for riding, are fast and nimble, while still others mainly provide milk. The Āl Murrah keep all three types, but their milk camels, most of which are black or dark brown in color, are their most valued possessions. The Āl 'Azab claim to have taken most of these, which are purebreds and known as *ash-Shuruf*, from the Mutayr tribe in raids against them during the last century. Their riding camels are all light tan in color and were taken in raids against tribes in Oman.

Āl 'Azab herds vary between forty and seventy-five full grown she-camels, with the average around fifty. These she-camels are the major concern of the herders and are divided into three groups for the purposes of herding. The first group comprises those with new-born calves. This group requires the most attention since the young calves cannot move rapidly at first. The mother camel must drink at least once a week, even in winter, unless the grasses are unusually green and plentiful. The Āl 'Azab do not allow their camels to breed until after the summer, and the calves are consequently born in late fall or early winter, following a twelve-month gestation.

The milk of these camels is rich and plentiful and deemed especially sweet by the Bedouin. At least one person, usually the eldest teen-aged son, is entrusted with herding this group while they graze. The mother camels and their young stay close by the tent. During the course of the day, the herder can expect to be visited by his father, grandfather, and some of the children, all of whom walk out to enjoy seeing the famous camels eating grass while their young frisk about. A long drink of superb frothy milk is always a major feature of these visits.

The second group of she-camels includes those which are still in milk and have unweaned young between the ages of eight months and a year and a half. They provide less-sweet milk, although in the case of the purebreds, it is still plentiful. These camels can move much faster than the others, since their young are more mobile. Another person, usually a teen-aged son, a young man, or a young unmarried daughter, is entrusted with this part of the herd. During the course of the day, this group moves farther afield from the tent. During exceptional years when grazing is unusually sparse, this group may be separated from the main herd for several weeks during the winter and spring while one or two youths take them in search of good grazing.

Pregnant camels make up the third division of the she-camels. They are left to wander by themselves during the day, but someone goes to drive them back to camp just before sunset.

The fourth group includes the male camels used as carriers and riding camels. The carriers number between twenty and thirty-five and include a single stud camel which characteristically belongs to the senior woman of the household. The carriers, which transport the tent, household items, and water, are ridden by the women during migration. The riding camels, most of which are females, are ridden by the men and youths during migration and as part of their herding activities. When not in use, both the carriers and the riding camels are hobbled and left to graze on their own. A woman or young girl goes out to fetch them whenever they are needed.

An average herd requires the attention of at least two full-time and one part-time herders. Altogether the nine household-herding units of the Āl Kurbi, a subdivision of the Āl 'Azab, have twenty full-time herders. (Eleven are unmarried males between the ages of eighteen and twenty-two. Six are married males in their twenties, three of whom are heads of households. Three are unmarried females about eighteen years old.) All young boys work part-time in herding. Those males who do not engage actively in herding include nine members of the senior generation and two young men who work full-time as wage laborers. None of the adult females work in the herding of camels. The nine households of the Āl Kurbi have a total population of sixty-four people.

The men do the milking at night with the occasional help of the younger women of the household. After grazing during the day, the camels are herded back to the camp about one hour after sunset. They are bedded down and begin chewing their cuds. An hour or two later, the she-camels with milk are roused one at a time and the woolen protector which is placed over their udders during the day is removed so their young can suckle. They are then milked into large enamel bowls that are brought back to the tent. Part of the milk is consumed at night while a greater part is left for the following morning. After they are milked, the camels once again are bedded down and continue chewing their cuds and dozing throughout the night.

Just before dawn everyone awakens to one of the old men singing the Muslim call to prayer. By sunrise the camels begin to get up. For several hours they stay within sight of the tent while one of the part-time herders watches them and begins to separate them into the four herding units. Each group is herded in a different direction. By mid-morning, the full-time herders leave the camp, usually on foot and armed with their highly valued rifles, and go to join their herds for the rest of the day.

The same pattern of activity occurs whether the camps are stationary or moving within a general area. If the camp is moving, the women load the tent and household items after mid-morning and depart for another campsite where they are joined in the early evening by the herd. During migrations from one area to another, as between fall and winter pasture areas, the rhythm of movement is much more intense and grazing en route is less important than getting the herds and households to their destinations. During summer months, the camels are abandoned to find their own grazing while their owners await their habitual return every four days to the wells where they are watered and milked.

SEASONAL RHYTHM OF HERDING

During the course of a yearly cycle, the Āl Murrah move over a vast expanse of territory. The Āl 'Azab, one of the most wide-ranging groups, migrate from their summer camps to fall pastures that lie some 200 miles to the southwest. Winter and spring pastures lie as far as 600 miles from the fall pastures. Thus, under normal circumstances, the Āl 'Azab travel a minimum of 1,200 miles per year, from home base to fall, winter, and spring pastures and back again to home base at their wells during the summer. This estimate does not include the milling around that occurs in each seasonal pasture area or travel spent in scouting for new pasture areas, in search of stray camels, in hunting, or in going to the urban centers to attend to market, political, and Reserve National Guard business. During the first year I spent with the Āl Murrah, I estimate that I traveled a minimum of 3,000 miles with them, exclusive of several trips to Riyadh and Taif in conjunction with problems related to my permission to conduct research.

Seasons

The Āl Murrah herding year is divided into four or sometimes five different periods. The number of periods and the precise beginning and end of each depends on when and how much rain falls. *Al-asferi*, the fall, begins in mid-September and lasts until December or early January. *Ash-shita*, the winter, follows and, in years of good mid-fall rains, the Bedouin enjoy a season they call *ar-rabi'ah* for a few weeks in February and early March. *As-seif* runs from late March to early June. The last period of the year is *al-gaidh*, the halting, at summer wells. Each season is associated with different pasture areas.

The yearly cycle of seasons includes two large-scale migrations, but the precise time and routes vary widely from year to year. Different units of social organization vary in importance according to the seasons, although the individual household remains autonomous throughout. Lineage members who share summer wells drift off toward fall pastures in mid-September. The move in December or January requires, on the other hand, a fast, intense migration northward over a minimum of 400 miles to the winter pastures. Throughout the fall grazing and during the migration northward, lineage members tend to graze the same general area and to follow similar tracks in their migration, although there is no strict coordination and lineages sometimes separate.

Winter pasturing and *ar-rabi'ah,* when it occurs, are periods in which lineages, clans, and tribes mix together. The nomads from the Rub' al-Khali also have a greater chance of coming in contact with sedentary villagers and urbanites during these periods in the north. An increased amount of feasting occurs, as *bayts* from different lineages and clans meet and invite each other to meals and coffee and tea sessions. They listen to the news and gossip of each group and talk at length about the state of the pastures and of the herds.

The winter is also the period when the shaikhs of the Āl Murrah make special trips into the desert and are feted, in partial return for the hospitality they dispense from their own tents which are usually located closer to settlements. Some of the princes of the royal families of Saudi Arabia and of the Arabian Gulf states also visit the desert during this period to hunt and to visit with the Bedouin. The winter and *ar-rabi'ah* are, thus, periods for reaffirming clan and tribal affiliations and vertical ties between shaikhs and tribespeople and between the royal families and the tribes. The complexity of desert society stands out most obviously during this period.

Late spring brings a return migration toward the south, although this is seldom as fast or as intense as the migration to winter pastures. Individual households seem to drift southward rather than deliberately move homeward. By early June, however, the herds and the Bedouin are at their summer wells. During the summer, the amount of water available determines whether the clan, the full lineage, or subdivisions of the lineage stays together. At the big oasis of Jabrin, the Āl Jaber clan summers together. Otherwise, lineages form the basis of most summer camps.

I cannot stress too much the flexibility and consequent variability of this system. No year exactly repeats itself. The most stable social units on a long-term basis are the summer camps, but even these vary from year to year. Political coalitions that form as a result of conflicts add another important dimension to Āl Murrah social life that we only mention in passing. Although many conflicts result from disputes over wells, they seldom disrupt the rhythm of herding. In order to understand more fully the ecological aspects of the interplay between Āl Murrah social structure and the pastoral exploitation of the desert, let us look more closely at each season.

The fall

After the long, scorching days of summer, September brings a marked change in temperature. The days are noticeably shorter, and by mid-September, noon temperatures seldom rise above 95° (Fahrenheit)—a considerable decrease from the 120° (Fahrenheit) of the summer. The camels no longer need water every four days. As a result, each household begins to leave the summer camp on its own accord to seek grazing farther from the wells. The actual moment of departure depends on when one's camels happen to come in to drink. Although there is no formal coordination, all those who have camped together and are from the same lineage head for the same general area.

Most of the Āl 'Azab and others such as the Āl Uwair of the Āl Ghurfran clan go to fall pastures deep inside the Rub' al-Khali. The weather is temperate during this season and they leave their tents and heavier household items at the summer wells. They take only a *hema,* a tent wall, with them for protection from the midday sun and wind and for privacy at night. Married couples and unmarried girls sleep by the side of one of these tent walls, which are arranged in a semi-circle to make an enclosure. Unmarried youths and male visitors, like myself, sleep in the open under the stars.

The density of population is at its lowest during this period. During the fall of 1968, 40 households operated in an area of approximately 4,000 square miles. Each household usually operates alone during this period. Dried clumps of grass, which are sparse and highly scattered, provide grazing, so the pastoralists spread out to take advantage of as much territory as possible. Throughout this season each household makes short moves that average about 7 miles every 2 days.

During the fall and throughout the rest of the herding year, several households often unite and move around together for periods that vary in time from a few days to several months. When this occurs, the Āl Murrah say they share a common *dar*, homestead, and special relationships exist between them, although each *bayt*, household or tent, remains autonomous. The members of a common *dar* are *gasir*, neighbors, to each other and are bound to defend each other against the attack even of one's close blood relatives. During the fall of 1968, about half of the Āl 'Azab joined in two and three household unit *dars* as they grazed an area some 200 miles southwest of their summer camp at Bir Fadhil. The closest water well was at Rayda, 75 miles away. Most of the *dars* were located in valleys between sand dunes where *abal* bushes and long-stemmed grasses were concentrated. The rest of the households operated alone on the flat plains of Rayda and Abu-Bahr, where clumps of dry grass grew and from which one could see only the faint white line of a sand dune some fifteen miles away.

The camels grazed near the camps for seven-day periods without drinking. On each eighth day, two youths or a young man and a girl traveled for two days with the herds to let them drink at a modern government-operated well at Rayda and to obtain water in big rubber innertubes for household uses, before traveling two more days on the return trip. Before this well was dug as part of the oil exploration activities of the Arabian American Oil Company (ARAMCO), the Āl 'Azab had to return to their own well at Bir Fadhil, a trip that required at least six days. When they are in the Rayda area, the nomads themselves seldom drink water but rely mostly on camel's milk for their liquid intake.

Whether the Āl 'Azab go to Rayda depends on whether rains have fallen there in previous years. A slight rain fell there in the late spring of 1968 and they grazed this area during the following fall. No rains at all fell there during the winter of 1969 and they did not go there during the fall of that year, although grasses and bushes still remained in that area. During the fall of 1969, they grazed an area closer to Bir Fadhil, which had received an especially good rain during the spring.

Both of these fall seasons, 1968 and 1969, were exciting to the Āl 'Azab. Their spirits were high because the grazing was more than adequate, the camels were in excellent shape, and there appeared to be an increase in the gazelle population of the northern Rub' al-Khali. Gazelle, oryx, and ostriches, among other wild animals, used to abound throughout much of desert Arabia. Only small herds of gazelle now remain in isolated regions such as the Rub' al-Khali, and the Āl Murrah were happy to see them on the increase.

Hunting gazelle is now a crime punishable by at least one year in prison in Saudi Arabia. In the 1950s and early 1960s, however, huge herds of wild animals were decimated, mainly by urban hunters who machine-gunned them from pickup trucks that raced after them in the desert. Few Saudi Arabians participate in this kind of activity nowadays, although we knew of parties of wealthy people from the Arabian Gulf states who illegally went hunting in the Rub' al-Khali during the fall and winter. Other Bedouin accompanied the urbanites in their wasteful kills in the name of sport—sometimes hundreds of carcasses were left to rot—but the Āl 'Azab abhored this practice. They, like the rest of the Āl Murrah, have been keen hunters who tracked and followed animals for days before they would make a kill for an occasional bit of meat. Today, they resent the restrictions placed on hunting because of the action of others who hunted and killed for joy alone.

Migration to winter pastures

To the Āl 'Azab, fall pasturing deep inside the Rub' al-Khali is a time of happiness and contentment. They always say it is the best season. There is the excitement of game to be hunted; there is the absence of the influences of the city, of the oasis, of the central government; there is bound to be relatively good grazing. But by November, the herders begin to scan the northern skies at night in hope of seeing flashes of lightning in the distant skies. *Insh'allah*, If Allah wills, the rains will come.

How long the fall grazing lasts depends on when and what kinds of rains fall in the north. In 1968, the rains began in early November, and the Āl 'Azab began their migration north during the first week of December. The following year slight rains began to fall only in mid-December, and the Āl 'Azab did not begin their trek until the first of January.

Throughout the late fall, the herdsmen are keenly interested in news about the rains. Word is brought about once a month by the members of the Reserve National Guard, who travel by truck to Abquaiq, the headquarters of the amir of the Āl Murrah. While in Abquaiq, they obtain as much and as precise information as possible from other members of the Āl Murrah who have been in the north or who have been in touch with other tribesmen in the north. Each person who reports rains is carefully questioned about how he obtained his information, whether it is first-hand or based on the reports of others. If there is any doubt about the reports (and many people get carried away when talking about the rains and sometimes tend to exaggerate), they ask the amir for his opinion. He is in a position to hear the reports of a wide range of tribesmen, and he considers it part of his business to provide information as reliable as possible for the herdsmen, although they recognize that they alone are responsible for the decisions they make about migration.

Conflicting reports occur most often during years in which the rains have been slight and scattered, as in the fall of 1969. In order to verify the exact situation, the amir sent al-Kurbi (my host and guide) and his father's brother in my truck on a reconnaissance mission to the northeast. They found that good but scattered rains had fallen only in the area of the Iraqi border. This they reported to the chief during a brief night visit at his tents in the desert outside of Abquaiq. They stopped to pick me up in the old Bedouin section of al-Hasa around midnight, and together we drove south 400 miles into the Rub' al-Khali to give the news to the Āl 'Azab and to any others we happened to meet. Within a day of our return to the herds, the migration north was in full swing.

Any time after the first of December and when reliable news establishes that rains have fallen in the north, each Āl 'Azab household changes the rhythm of its movements. Instead of short moves every few days within a given area, the camels are herded back toward Bir Fadhil in marches that last from about two hours after sunrise until around sunset, with the camels grazing for a few hours near the camp after sunset.

Depending on how cold the weather is, either tents or enclosure walls are set up about an hour before sunset. The herds graze for a couple of hours and arrive just after dark, at which time they are milked. Camp fires glow in the men's sections of the tents or in front of the enclosures, and one hears the ringing beat of coffee beans being pounded into powder in heavy brass mortars. The men and youths gather closely around the fires and talk of what and whom they have seen during the day. Some have probably talked with members of other lineages and clans with whom they exchanged greetings and news. Mention of these encounters brings the old men to reminisce about the other lineages and to talk about raids and wars in which they participated in the old days. The men eat a communal meal of rice about three hours after sunset. They drink milk later on, and most of the youths sit up until well past midnight talking about camels and the state of the grazing, reciting poems, and listening to the Bedouin Hour on Radio Kuwait. All too soon, the morning call to prayer comes, just before sunrise, and a new day begins as the march goes on toward the north.

Migrations to winter pasture last from ten to fifteen days after departure from Bir Fadhil. Each day a distance between thirty and forty miles is covered. The same general trajectory is followed by an Āl 'Azab units, and jocular competition takes place between the different units as they race to the north. The Āl 'Azab usually move north through the Summan just to the east of the Dahna. They generally water their camels at the westernmost wells at Haradh. In 1970, however, they had to hire privately-owned tankers to truck water to their herds, since they thought the development works at the King Faisal Settlement Project, once intended mainly to make the Āl Murrah settle in one place, would excite their camels too much. The camels drink again at the government-operated well at al-Khurais, and within a few days, the Āl 'Azab reach the site of their usual winter pasture areas.

Other lineages of the Āl Murrah participate in similar migrations from their fall pastures and the site of their summer camps. Most treks are shorter than those of the Āl 'Azab. Some lineages are increasingly uniting to hire big trucks to carry their household items and the women to the northern pastures. In 1970, for example, 24 households of the Āl Gathban lineage of the Āl Jaber clan did this at a cost of 70 Saudi Arabian riyals (then $16) per household. This joint action, however, represents the only co-ordinated migratory action taken by a descent group. Unlike the highly organized migrations of many Iranian nomads and of other Bedouin who cross nontribal territory, the Āl Murrah trips are more or less piecemeal affairs, with each *bayt* responsible for itself and joining together with other *bayts* in a *dar* only for momentary convenience and companionship.

The winter and *ar-rabi'ah*

The location of winter pastures varies each year. Late fall and winter rains are usually limited to particular localities and result in winter grasses coming up at different times and in different places. The Āl Murrah say they take their camels anywhere in the entire Arabian Peninsula and as far north as Damascus in search of winter grazing. The areas they normally exploit, however, lie immediately to the north of the al-Hasa oasis, extend as far north as Kuwait and southern Iraq, and include the Dahna on the west. In unusual years, when there is little vegetation in this area, some of the Āl Murrah (and especially the Āl 'Azab) migrate across the Dahna into central Najd as far west as Dawadimi. When prolonged droughts occur throughout northern Arabia, the Āl 'Azab and other Āl Murrah based in the Rub' al-Khali spend the winters in southern Arabia near Najran.

None of the winter pastures areas are included in *dirat-Āl Murrah*, Āl Murrah territories. All of them lie outside their own traditional territories. Nowhere to the north of al-Hasa do the Āl Murrah have any wells of their own. Other tribes are based in these areas, and the wells and oases that dot the north belong to them. Government-operated wells now exist in this area and all tribes have equal rights of access to them. In the past, however, the Āl Murrah and any other tribes traveling to these areas for winter pasture had to depend on good relations with the tribes there for at least a part of their water supply, although this may be minimal during the winter season.

The winter grasses contain a considerable amount of moisture which camels can absorb. Temperatures are mild, which lessens the need for the camels to drink. Rain water collects in ponds and is sought by the herdsmen, who value it above the purest well water as being a direct gift from God. In especially good years, when the winter grasses are very green and there have been good rains, the Āl Murrah have no pressing need for access to wells.

The Āl Murrah do not ask anyone's permission to pasture their camels in the north. Any area that has vegetation and is not already occupied is acceptable, and I know of no instance in which any of the tribes of northern Arabia challenged their right to these pastures. Prior to the establishment of the modern Kingdom of Saudi Arabia, during the first three decades of this century, camel raiding was practiced throughout this area and the Āl Murrah were subject to raids when they were outside their own tribal territories. They claim, however, that the balance was always in their favor and that they enriched their herds by raids against all the major tribes of the north, especially the Mutayr, during the latter part of the nineteenth century.

Special relations exist between the Āl Murrah and only one of the major tribes of northeastern Arabia, the Āl 'Ajman. Both consider themselves *ayal 'amm*, father's brother's sons, since both are descendants of Yam. Both Āl 'Ajman and Āl Murrah traditionally used to raid each other, but they unite in case of attack against either by another group. The Āl Murrah can thus count on support and access to Āl 'Ajman wells in case of conflicts with other tribes, such as the Mutayr or the Subai', who predominate in the northeast along with the Āl 'Ajman. Both the Āl Murrah and the Āl 'Ajman have close tribal relatives in the Najran area in southwestern Arabia, who guarantee both tribes access to pastures and wells in that area. In recent decades, however, no major conflicts have arisen between the Āl Murrah and any other tribes over access to wells or winter pasture areas. Nowadays, the existence of government-operated wells practically ends any concern over water rights, since complete dependence on the wells of other tribes no longer exists.

When good fresh winter pastures are found, the Bedouin enjoy a period called *ar-rabi'ah*. Depending on the state of the pasturage, this lasts from about six to ten weeks from January on. During years in which rainfall is slight and there is little fresh pasturage, the Bedouin simply spend the winter, *ash-shita*, grazing last year's grasses and bushes and do not enjoy *ar-rabi'ah*. When there is *ar-rabi'ah*, the Bedouin settle down to graze a single area; otherwise they continue to move widely in search of adequate grazing.

Once the nomads reach the area of their winter pastures, after about two weeks of moving every day, they settle down and begin

a pattern of movement that is similar to that of the fall. Households tend to join together in *dars* of two to four units and make
short moves of six to ten miles every three or four days. The
households that unite tend to be members of the same minimal
lineage but seldom include all such members. Marital ties are
important considerations behind the union of some *bayts* in a *dar*.
In some cases, however, no special ties of blood or marriage relate the households to each other. These *dars* can be formed either
during the migration north or in the winter pastures. They tend to
remain united until the end of the winter, although grazing conditions can lead to separation if there is a need to spread out
over a greater territory.

Except for the summer camps, the density of population is at
its highest during the winter months. If the pasturage is good, a
majority of at least five major Saudi Arabian tribes—the Āl
Murrah, the Āl 'Ajman, the Mutayr, the Subai', and the Dawasir—
converge on the same pasture areas of northeast Arabia. Shepherd
tribes of lower status than the camel nomads and gypsy tribes
also converge on the same area. The towns and oases which dot
this region add groups of peasants and merchants to the complexity.

The winter is an especially busy time for the herdsmen. The
Āl Murrah control the breeding of their animals so that young
camels are born during the late fall and winter. Herding camels
with young calves is more time-consuming than taking care of
the other divisions of the herd, although this extra work is performed with pleasure since the Bedouin highly value the milk
these camels produce. Also, camels stray easily during the winter,
and the youths spend a great deal of time tracking them down.
The herdsmen are keen to fatten their animals as much as possible
during the winter and take great care to search out the very best
grasses that have not already been grazed. The herds are kept
continuously on the move and seldom graze the same plot for
more than one day, except during periods of *ar-rabi'ah* when they
are more stationary.

Decisions about moving camp are arrived at by consensus of
the members of a *dar*. Every morning, just after the predawn
prayers and before the sun has risen, a coffee fire is started in
front of the men's section of every tent. The men sip a few cups
of coffee, eat two or three dates, and then pass the rest of the
coffee to the women. They drift over to the tent of the senior man

in the *dar* and again sip coffee and warm themselves around the fire. They discuss whether they should move, considering the status of the grasses they have been grazing and the number of different groups in the same area. Adult married sons take an active part in the discussion while the younger sons listen and occasionally add a note about the kinds of grasses they have seen in different areas. When a consensus is reached, if they are staying, they put more fuel on the fire to make more coffee and ginger-spiced hot milk, and if they are moving, the women (who have been listening from behind the *ru'ag*) begin to take down the tent. On a move, the women are in the saddle by four or five hours after sunrise and travel for about four hours before they dismount and pitch their tents. The herds graze slowly in the general direction of the new camps and are brought in at nightfall by the two or three herdsmen who have been with them.

The winter is not only a busy time for the herdsmen; household work also increases. The women are kept busy loading and unloading the camp equipment, of which there is much more than during the fall migration. A marked increase in feasting also occurs. Members of the same lineage who were separated during the migration from fall to winter pastures meet and decide to feast each other for periods of several days. In-laws commonly meet during winter pastures and they too feast each other. Visitors from other tribes and from different clans of the Āl Murrah pass by and are invited to special meals in their honor. As a result, the women spend increased amounts of time in the preparation of food.

The increased density of population during the winter season, the mixture of people from different lineages, clans, and tribes, and the availability of sheep for purchase all contribute to the increase in feasting. Each Āl Murrah household slaughters at least three or four new-born male camels each winter. None of the females are slaughtered unless they are obviously ill and seem incapable of surviving. They also purchase an equal number of sheep per household from shepherd tribes who graze their flocks in the same area. The prices they pay for a sheep are slightly higher than the prices they would pay for the same animal in an urban market where the supply of sheep for sale is greater.

The young men slaughter and skin the sheep. The animal is then boiled in a large caldron by the women, who add onions and spices to the water. The women prepare the rice, and when the meat is done, one of the men spreads the rice on a large circular tray at least four feet in diameter and then places the meat on top of the rice. The laden tray is taken to the men's section of the tent where the male guests gather and begin eating, using only their right hands since their left hands are considered unclean. Following Arab etiquette, the host refrains from eating until all his guests have satisfied themselves. Part of the meat, usually at least a shoulder and the ribs, are reserved for the host and the women of the tent. Tea, coffee, and dates, and the passing of incense precede and follow such meals.

The spring

In northern climates, spring is the season when life begins to stir and plants blossom. In the deserts of Arabia, although they lie north of the tropics, the spring brings not new life but rather the slowing down of all movement. Plants that were green during the winter begin to dry up and turn brown. Temperatures increase daily. In late March and April, hot sand storms blow up and last from one to five days, during which time people and animals are scorched amid swirls of burning sand. Visiting and feasting become less frequent, and the *dars* that have remained intact through the winter begin to break up, as individual *bayts* begin drifting back toward their lineage's well.

The Āl Murrah call this period *as-seif*, a term the sedentary people use for the summer rather than the spring. Long moves are undertaken during the return to the summer campsites, but seldom do the Āl Murrah hurry as much as during the move from fall to winter pastures. Herds are occasionally split up during this period as a lone herder, usually an unmarried male, takes as much as a third of the herd to graze separately from the rest. Before settling at summer camps, which occurs by the end of June at the latest, the Āl 'Azab stop at small wells they claim in an area slightly north of their main well at Bir Fadhil in the Rub' al-Khali. They camp in groups of five or six *bayts* at shallow wells during much of May and graze sand hills just to the north of the plains that separate the Rub' al-Khali from the rest of northern Arabia. Minimal lineages tend to cling together, but groups from other clans and lineages share these wells as they pass by on their way to their own wells.

The herdsmen continue to accompany the herds during the late spring days and drive the animals back to the camp every night, where they are milked and bedded down. Finally, in early June, as the daytime temperatures soar to 110° (Fahrenheit) and above, the tents are taken down and loaded on the carrier camels for the last time, and the nomads begin crossing the wide, barren plains. After two days they arrive at the summer wells, where they remain for a minimum of three months.

The summer

Much to my chagrin, during both summers (1968 and 1969) I spent in Saudi Arabia, the Āl 'Azab did not camp together, although they claim they always spend the summer at Bir Fadhil. After spending nine months migrating with units that never included more than four households and usually only one or two, I was eager to see all of the Āl 'Azab, who claim to be one united group, together. Not only did I look forward to getting to know some of the households better, but I hoped to see what their life was like when they were united in a single residential area for three months.

In 1968, however, work was initiated under the auspices of the Saudi Arabian Ministry of Agriculture and Water to modernize Bir Fadhil by cleaning it out and building concrete walls around the top third of the well. By the summer of 1969 this work had not been completed. Therefore the Āl 'Azab did not congregate there but, divided in three different groups, stayed at smaller wells, located ten to forty miles from Bir Fadhil. During both years, minimal lineages tended to remain together and to provide the basis for division of the Āl 'Azab camel herders. By the beginning of the summer of 1970, the repair work had still not been completed and only a part of the Āl 'Azab went to Bir Fadhil. I have been told by Āl Murrah friends whom I saw in 1972 that during 1971 the Āl 'Azab finally did camp there.

The unit that forms the basis for the majority of Āl Murrah summer camps is the maximal lineage. The entire Āl Jaber clan camps together at the date palm oasis of Jabrin, but even here different lineages occupy different parts of the oasis. The variability and flexibility so characteristic of the Āl Murrah during the fall, winter, and spring carries over into the summer. The main difference between the summer and the rest of the year lies in the herding patterns and in the highly concentrated population in summer camps. The groups that cluster together always include a core of closely related males, usually members of a single lineage, but some members of a lineage may be absent and a few members of other lineages may be present. Although the exact composition of summer camps seldom repeats itself from year to year, the members of a lineage do camp together frequently, if for no other reason than the fact that, according to the Āl Murrah, camels have a homing instinct that compels them to return to the same general area each summer. Indeed, camels lost or abandoned during winter pastures are said to return on their own to the wells of the lineage which owns them.

The state of pastures is not a major factor in choosing the location of a summer camp. The Āl 'Azab claim a number of small wells in the general vicinity of Bir Fadhil, and grazing conditions are sometimes taken into consideration in deciding whether to congregate at Bir Fadhil or to remain separated in smaller units nearby. But while grazing is the primary consideration during the fall, winter, and spring, water is the main problem during the summer. Camels are fattened as much as grazing conditions permit prior to the summer, during which time they are expected to survive on their own and to utilize the energy they have been able to store up in the fatty tissue in their humps.

After settling in at the summer camps, nobody herds the camels. They are watered at the well, milked, and left on their own to graze whatever grasses and bushes they can find. The herds remain united without the interference of herders and return by themselves to the well every four days. Each bayt waters its own camels and no cooperation, other than occasional token help in drawing water, takes place.

The wells the Āl 'Azab utilized in 1968, 1969, and 1970 varied between 20 and 60 feet in depth, although Bir Fadhil is approximately 150 feet deep. Water is drawn by attaching a leather bucket to a rope, the other end of which is tied to a wooden saddle on one of the carrier camels. The rope runs over a pulley between two poles which are placed on one side of the well. A girl rides the camel back and forth, which allows the bucket to descend into the well, fill, and then be pulled out. The camels crowd around an oval leather trough about four feet in diameter and two feet deep and drink the water that two young men pour into it from the bucket. Approximately two hours are spent watering the herd. After they have drunk, they are milked. After several more hours they are given a little more water and then they depart from the camp to graze. Milk continues to be plentiful during the summer, although it is not as rich as during the winter and spring when calves are newly born. It is shared among households, since fresh milk is only available once every four days during the summer.

SPECIALIZED KNOWLEDGE OF THE BEDOUIN

Traditionally, the sedentary people in Arabia have scoffed at the Bedouin as being silly, stupid, and rough-hewn. They see them as country-bumpkins and make jokes about their ignorance of sophisticated city ways and their difficulty in comprehending the complexities of a rapidly changing modern world. More serious criticism focuses on their lack of erudition in Islam. At the same time, the urbanites and villagers give numerous examples showing how intelligent and skilled the Bedouin are within their desert environment. Indeed, they marvel at the skills of the nomads and often attribute to them some special sense lacking among sedentary people.

Arabian cultiure embodies two contradictory currents of thought. One, stemming from the sedentary Arabs, is based on literacy; it includes an erudite knowledge of Islam and classical Arabic literature. The other stems from the nomadic desert Arabs, who in their simple tribal life embody the ideals of austerity, endurance, justice, and hospitality. In the past, many urban families sent their children to live among the Bedouin for a few seasons in order to learn the lore of the Bedouin and to absorb the positive values of living in a simple society in the purity of the desert with the camels. Even today, many members of the urban elites of Saudi Arabia and the Arabian Gulf states make trips to the desert to hunt and to sit with the Bedouin, who tell them stories of their nomadic life.

A conflict subsists, however, between the rough-hewn traditions and unlettered learning of the Bedouin and the refined classical knowledge of the traditional urbanite. Consider, for example, the experience of the future founder of modern Saudi Arabia, 'Abd al-Aziz ibn-Sa'ud, the father of King Faisal. When still a youth, he spent about two years as an exile living under the protection of the Āl Shoraim family of paramount chiefs of the Āl Murrah. He shared their simple diet of dates and camel's milk and is said to have participated in camel raids and in all aspects of their life. From this period, he is said to have gained his deep knowledge and feeling for Arab concepts of justice and egalitarianism that led him to become a highly successful arbitrator and decision-maker and, thereby, to forge peace in a land that had known little but wars and internecine feuding for generations. At the same time, he was supposedly revulsed by the general irreligiosity and ignorance of these long-haired, unkempt Bedouin, who seemed to understand little of the meaning of the prayers they repeated. He came to deplore their raiding of each other and to feel that a nomadic existence precluded a proper Muslim existence. Although he is described in history books as a desert king and is depicted in close association with the Bedouin, he, perhaps more than anyone else, set in motion the destruction of the traditional basis of their tribal life and began their incorporation into the Islamic-based Saudi state, a process we will discuss in greater detail in subsequent chapters.

Most of the skills and knowledge of the Bedouin are directly related to their herding activities, which require both a keen sense of observation and a wide knowledge of geographical features and of desert plants and animals. The average Bedouin also has a great depth of genealogical knowledge and can recite poetry and the *hadith* (or traditions) of the Arabs for hours on end. Not all Bedouin, however, are equally skilled at herding or knowledgeable about the geography and flora and fauna of the desert. The camel nomads are accredited as being the most knowledgeable, and those who inhabit the Rub' al-Khali are superior. I have often heard sheep and goat herding Bedouin speak of the Āl 'Azab and the other groups who frequent the Rub' al-Khali with awe, especially because of their somewhat uncanny skills at tracking animals, their vast geographical knowledge, and their reified senses of direction and observation.

The Āl Murrah are renowned as trackers. In the desert sands they easily identify the tracks of animals and of people. All the members of a *bayt* know the individual footprints of their own camels and at least some of the footprints of their kinsmen's camels. Thus any youth or adult can observe a set of footprints and tell whether any of his own camels are among them. This ability is particularly useful when searching for strayed camels, as well as in looking for one's *bayt* when one has been away and it has moved.

Any boy or girl can distinguish the tracks of all animals that live in desert Arabia. By the time they are in their teens, everybody can tell the length of time elapsed since the tracks were made, how many animals or people were involved, and point to certain characteristics of the individuals. For example, they can distinguish whether a set of human footprints are those of a woman or a man, whether the person is young or old, and if they are those of a woman, they can tell if she is pregnant. The same kind of information can be discerned from the tracks of camels.

Because of this ability, until recently, a number of Āl Murrah were attached as trackers to every major police station in Saudi Arabia. When a crime had been committed, the tracker went to the scene and observed the footprints in the area. Then he went and sat in the marketplace of the town or village to observe the feet of people in attendance at the market. The trackers are accredited with solving many cases in this fashion and their testimony in court was that of special witnesses. That they performed this function has not led to the greater popularity of the Āl Murrah among many sedentary Saudi Arabians. The latter's objections stem not so much from the Āl Murrah interfering with would-be criminals as in the extraordinariness of their ability to recognize a man by his feet and his footprints. Because of this seemingly extraordinary power, some suggest that the Āl Murrah have a special relationship with *jinns*. Nowadays, these services of the Āl Murrah are discontinued in all but a few traditional villages and towns—and anyway most urbanites now wear shoes.

Another skill that invites the description of extraordinary is their sense of direction. Many times I have traveled with the Āl Murrah across the flat, featureless plains that lie across the northern face of the Rub' al-Khali and have been amazed by their ability to arrive after as much as a whole day's travel at precisely the place they intended to reach, although there are practically no landmarks. Oftentimes I drove while al-Kurbi and other passengers dozed. Whenever they awoke, they would immediately correct my course without any pause. Other Bedouin from other tribes often rode with us during the winter season in the north and were always amazed by the Āl Murrah's ability not to get lost and to keep on a direct course of travel, even when hills and other geographical features had to be circumnavigated. Most of the northern Bedouin nowadays travel almost exclusively on well-established desert trails, even within their own tribe's traditional territory.

Coupled with their sense of direction is a vast amount of geographical knowledge. Older men among the Āl Murrah have detailed knowledge about most of the Arabian Peninsula, an area as large as one third of the United States. Naturally, they know their own tribal territory, but at one time or another they have visited almost every part of desert Arabia. Some of their travels have been in conjunction with herding, while others have been as participants in raiding parties or as members of the Muslim Brotherhood armies during the second and third decades of this century. Younger men, who have participated less in military activities which used to carry men far afield, have less knowledge than the old men, but they still know a great deal. Whenever they travel, the Āl Murrah are careful observers of the land, the plants that grow there, the location of wells, and the people who live there.

Every major feature in the landscape of Arabia is given a proper name, as well as being classified as being a member of a certain type of general phenomena. Thus they recognize such general features as wadis, sand dunes, sand hills, mountains, and gravel plains by the use of a generalized term for each. They also single out each individual wadi or sand dune by a proper name. Every adult and most youths know the names and locations of all these features which fall within Āl Murrah territories and in northeastern Arabia, although those who do not live in the Rub' al-Khali are somewhat vague about the precise location of some places there. This knowledge is particularly evident during the late fall when they begin to gather information about the rains. They have to be sure of the precise location of each rain, as this determines the site of their winter pastures.

They also know the types of grasses and bushes that grow in each area and are capable of recognizing by name all of the different species of plants that grow in the territories they frequent. They are keenly interested in plants and continuously tried to teach me the names of every variety of plants they recognize and to tell me its characteristics. Unfortunately, I was a rebellious student and only mastered the Arabic names of a few of the most important and common plants. A specific study of both ethnogeography and ethnobotany among the Āl Murrah would surely provide an amazingly large quantity of items and would enrich our knowledge of basic technical aspects of desert and steppe pastoralism.

As mentioned earlier, camels are the abiding passion of the Āl Murrah. Even when other subjects are discussed, camels always seem to creep into the conversation. Linguists have often noted that the Arabic language possesses an extremely large number of words that mean camel and that many different varieties and aspects of camels are distinguished through the use of different words. A large number of words are used to refer to any given camel, depending on the specific aspect of its individuality one wants to express. The Āl Murrah use different terms depending on whether they want to stress the sex, age, color, use, or breed of the animal. Thus there are at least five different terms that can be used to single out any camel. Each camel is also given a proper name and its genealogy is traced through the female line—for as many as ten generations in the case of some of their most famous purebreds. Similar genealogies were also known for the horses they kept mainly for raiding and warfare before ibn-Saʻud convinced them to give them up as being unnecessary in a peaceful society. The Āl Murrah also consider themselves capable of curing sick camels by a special process of cauterization, in which they use a hot iron to burn different parts of the animal according to the disease it has.

The specialized knowledge and skills the Āl Murrah possess can all be explained in relation to their habitation of the desert. All of them are practical and necessary for the successful exploitation of its resources. The desert environment also encourages a heightened sense of observation and awareness that is often lacking in villagers and urbanites. The Bedouin live most of their lives outside and are in close association with their animals. Thus while it is necessary to be able to track strayed camels, it is easy for one accustomed to living in sandy areas with the same animals for years to recognize individual characteristics of their footprints. The wide open spaces of the Rub' al-Khali also condition one to scan great distances and to recognize what appear as minute specks on the horizon as camels, tents, or whatever. The stars are there every night of the year for everyone to see, and it is not difficult to understand how the Bedouin can tell the seasons and the time at night by looking at the heavens. They learn what they know from experience and from listening to the talk of their elders. There are no schools and no initiations into the lore of the tribe. They learn by immersion in their environment. They reject the notion held by some sedentary Arabs that they have any special senses or that they are in touch with *jinns* or any other extraordinary powers. Their subsistence and their survival depend on their own skills in exploiting a harsh and demanding physical environment. Their knowledge of it is practical, not esoteric.

Chapter 3

THE HOUSEHOLD, MARRIAGE, AND FAMILY LIFE

Throughout most of the year, the households of the Āl Murrah are located deep within the desert. To travel to them requires the services of a guide and one of the first things I had to do in beginning my research was to find a guide. During the first few weeks I spent visiting the amir of the Āl Murrah in his head-quarters in Abquaiq, I met a man slightly over thirty. He was a member of the Reserve National Guard and he told me that his and his father's tent and their camels were deep inside the Rub' al-Khali. He had worked for several years in Kuwait and with his savings had just bought a used pickup truck, which he was planning to use in desert hauling for hire. I told him that I had been promised the use of a pickup truck by the Saudi Arabian Royal Ministry of Agriculture and Water and that I was looking for a driver-guide. He immediately responded that he was the man for the job and we went together to seek the amir's approval. The amir was highly enthusiastic and told me that this man's lineage was one of the most traditional and most famous groups of camel nomads in Arabia. They have some of the best herds and they habitually migrate deep inside the Rub' al-Khali in search of the best grazing. This man, al-Kurbi, thus became my guide, companion, and friend throughout the eighteen months I lived among the Āl Murrah.

At the end of September, 1968, when al-Kurbi and the rest of the Āl Murrah Reserve National Guardsmen received their salaries and finished their duties, we left Abquaiq in al-Kurbi's truck and traveled to Hofuf, the market and administrative center of al-Hasa oasis. We spent the night camping in the outskirts of town and then spent the next day in the market. With the money he had just received (250 Saudi Arabian riyals, $55 in 1968), al-Kurbi bought rice, dates, coffee beans, tea, sugar, cardamom, perfume, incense, and a few articles of clothing for his and his elder brother's young sons. In the late afternoon, we loaded the truck with these purchases and those of four men of the Āl Jaber clan. These men, along with al-Kurbi's wife who had come to see a doctor in Hofuf, his paternal uncle who is also his wife's father, a man from his own lineage, and three women from the Āl Jaber climbed aboard and we departed just after the sunset prayers.

Around midnight, after traveling south on a rough desert track, we stopped and slept on a bare rocky plain. Before dawn, the temperature near freezing, we awoke for the morning prayers, made coffee, and ate some dates. We then drove an hour and a half until we saw three small black tents pitched together at the foot of a small hill. These were the tents of our Āl Jaber companions. They unloaded their belongings, invited us to coffee and tea, and gave us camel's milk to drink. One of the men paid al-Kurbi 25 riyals ($5.50) for his transportation services, and we departed.

We continued southward and after an hour saw in the distance the palm groves of Jabrin, the last oasis before the Rub' al-Khali. The track we had been on became more faint and we soon left it to travel cross-country. By noon, we were traveling southwestward across the wide Abu-Bahr plain, navigating through occasional sand islands and sand hills. We stopped at the edge of a sand dune, gathered firewood from dead bushes and made a fire to cook a pot of rice and to brew coffee. We napped in the shade of the truck and then, after praying the afternoon prayers, continued on until sunset when we stopped to pray again, and then went on for about three more hours. Since we had left the Āl Jaber, we had not seen any tents, any camels, or any trace of human life, although we had traveled 300 miles across wide open country.

We were exhausted—at least I was—and we stopped to sleep, this time in comfortable sand rather than on the hard rocky plain as during the night before. The next morning we arose, once again just before dawn, and continued our trip. Soon, we spotted some camels' tracks, and al-Kurbi and the others got out to look at them. His paternal uncle recognized some of them as those of his brother's camels and said they were from yesterday. They noticed the direction the camels were going and all decided that we would find 'arabna, our Arabs, just beyond a long dune on the horizon to the south.

We headed in that direction, navigated around the end of the dune, and came into a sandy area with some camels grazing on dried clumps of grasses and abal bushes. Two youths with shoulder-length hair and armed with rifles were with the camels. We drove over to them, got out of the truck, greeted them, and asked them where the Arabs were. One of the youths, Hurran, came with us and we soon arrived at three black tents camped together on a sand hill. One of these belonged to al-Kurbi's lineage mate who was traveling with us. He invited us to coffee, tea, camel's milk, dates, and a meal of rice.

Al-Kurbi and his paternal uncle discussed the news of their trip to Abquaiq with several men who had gathered for coffee. They asked who I was and al-Kurbi explained that I was his brother who had come to live in the desert. I told them that I was a university student and had come to write a book about the Āl Murrah and their customs for my doctoral degree. Hurran, one of the youths we had met in the morning, brought his riding camel and told me to ride around the camp. Then he challenged me to a foot race, which he graciously let me win. He brought his rifle, set up a target and asked me to try my luck, which was good that day. All this took place in front of a group of women who sat apart from the men in another tent watching through slits in their black mask-like veils. Hurran said we would be friends, that he would teach me how to be a Bedouin and that we would go with the camels and look for banat al-hawa, daughters of the wind. But his family decided to go north and I did not see them again until seven months later, although they were from the same lineage as al-Kurbi.

In midafternoon, al-Kurbi, his wife, and his paternal uncle and I continued our trip. We traveled about fifteen more miles until we came on a vast plain with scattered clumps of grass and only a single sand dune on the horizon to break the monotony. We stopped and scanned the horizon. Al-Kurbi spotted a small black speck, his father's camp, alone in this vastness, with their camels grazing around it. Soon I was being introduced to all his family—his father, 'Ali; his mother, bint Rajah; two brothers, Muhammad and Merzuq; Muhammad's wife, bint al-Kurbi; and his son, Batahan. His elder brother, Rajah, had his own tent and was working as a guard at an oil installation in the north. His paternal uncle stayed on for a while here because his wife had died and he didn't have a tent of his own.

Throughout my stay with the Āl Murrah, al-Kurbi's father's household was my place of residence. For eighteen months I migrated with them, helped herd their camels, made coffee in their tent, and helped them gather firewood. I came to know them almost as my own family, and as al-Kurbi's brother, Muhammad, once put it, "You don't have to worry about anything. We are your brothers, and if anyone wrongs you, we will seek revenge."

Throughout the fall of 1968, our household stayed by itself. Merzuq took me herding and began teaching me the names and types of the camels, the names of different grasses and bushes, and talked a great deal about hunting. It was fun and I felt really close to these people, but I also felt frustrated. I had come to study a tribe and here I was with only one household. I wanted to meet at least the rest of al-Kurbi's lineage, the Āl 'Azab, but the nearest tents were at least fifteen miles away and we had little gasoline to waste on trips which they considered unnecessary. In time, however, I came to appreciate the importance of the household as a basic unit in Āl Murrah economy and society. A high degree of dispersal is a major fact of Āl Murrah social life, and although they speak a great deal about how they are all brothers and all one people, they spend much of their life in solitary independence or in the company of only one to three other households.

THE TENT-HOUSEHOLD

The Āl Murrah use the term *bayt* to mean both household and tent. *Bayt,* in its meaning of tent, is contrasted with *gasr,* which refers to the edifice in which sedentary folk reside, although *bayt*, in its meaning of household, is used equally to refer to the social unit which resides in both the tent and the permanent house. They also use a word, *dar*, that is usually glossed in English as house but which among them refers to *homestead*, i.e., the *bayt* itself and the area immediately surrounding it. Two or more *bayts* that camp and migrate together occupy a single *dar*. Special relationships exist among the members of a *dar* for the duration of the time they are united. Each *bayt* occupies the category of *gasir*, neighbor, to the other, and this bond overrides all considerations of either blood or marital relationships. A man defends his *gasir* against the attack of even his closest male relatives.

Blood relationship is never given as a reason for uniting *bayts* in a common *dar*, although the members of *dar* are often close blood relatives. Marital ties, however, quite often influence the formation of *dars*, especially when a marriage has occurred between members of different lineages. In such cases, a man makes an effort to unite his *bayt* with that of his father-in-law or brothers-in-law so that his wife can have an opportunity to visit with her relatives. Friendship and habit are minor factors influencing the union of *bayts* in a *dar*.

When united in a *dar*, each *bayt* continues to function as an independent social and economic unit; there is no division of labor between *bayts* in the *dar* with regard to herding activities. Coffee and tea are dispersed equally among tents and most men and women make the rounds of all the *bayts* in the *dar* during the course of the day. The major cooked meal of the day is usually communal for all the males of the *dar* and responsibility shifts from one *bayt* to another, although no strict accounting is kept.

No major economic incentive compels people to unite in a *dar*. Chance meetings in the course of migration are probably the major consideration. Two or three (seldom more than four) *bayts* that happen to be grazing their herds in similar areas decide informally to stay together. As the pasturage changes, there is no hesitation about splitting up. A desire for companionship is an underlying factor, so that in a kinship-oriented society like that of the Āl Murrah, most *dars* are composed of close relatives. In rare instances, protection is the major consideration; if a murder has been committed, the murderer joins his *bayt* in forming a *dar* with another *bayt* that is bound by custom to provide protection for a year and a day.

Each *bayt* is identified by the name of the senior male who resides in it, as *bayt Āl 'Ali*, tent or household of the People of 'Ali. The tent itself belongs to the senior woman. Traditionally, this woman and her daughters and daughters-in-law wove the tent themselves out of goat's hair they collected. Nowadays, tents are more often machine-made and purchased for cash in market towns. An average-sized tent costs about 4,500 riyals ($1,000 in 1968–70), but few people buy a complete tent at one time. Strips of machine-woven black goat's hair are purchased as they are needed and then put together by the women to construct their tent or repair an older one. The actual cash for such materials is provided by the male or males of the household, but the tent is still referred to as belonging to the woman.

In spite of the increasing incidence of purchasing tent materials that has followed in the wake of the developing oil industry, weaving continues to be a major concern of the women, and some essential items of the tent, such as the walls and the *ru'ag*, a tapestry-like divider between the men's and women's sections, are still homemade and employ designs peculiar to the tribe and the lineage. The tent is the exclusive responsibility of the women, who take it down, fold it, transport it, and set it up again. Furthermore, no man ever lives either alone or with other men in any tent without a woman, although occasionally a divorced or widowed woman lives alone with her children. A single man always resides in someone else's tent.

In contrast to the tents of many sheep herders, those of the Āl Murrah are rather small. As camel herders, they move fast and often, and large and cumbersome household items would be a burden. Most have two or three center poles; only five or six families, three of them of amir status, have four-poled tents; only one, that of the wife of the previous amir, has five poles. They are always pitched facing south. The men's section occupies one-fourth to one-third of the east end. This is the only area that a male visitor approaches and it is the scene of all male social activities. The women's section is subdivided by piling up household items and supplies in such a way that each conjugal unit has a separate place in the tent. Every married woman has one of these subdivisions as her own and it is here that she, her husband, and their young children sleep at night. Male guests and all males past puberty sleep in the men's section. The fire on which the women prepare meals, as well as the coffee and tea for their own socializing, is located at the southwest corner of the tent or just outside it. The men's coffee fire is located just in front of their section. See Figure 3.

All but a few Āl Murrah households are composed of more than one conjugal family. Most include three generations of males —grandfather, father, and grandson—and their wives. The household in which I lived was composed of three conjugal families. These included 'Ali, an elderly man of about seventy who was the head of the household, and his wife, bint Rajah. Their second eldest son, his wife, and their young son also lived in this unit. An unmarried son about twenty also resided here. The only daughter of 'Ali and bint Rajah had married and left this household to live with her husband. The eldest son of the family, Rajah, established his own independent household and received a portion

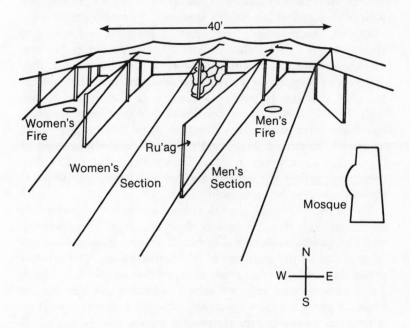

Figure 3. The tent.

of the herd as his own during the time I lived among them. Prior to receiving his part of the herd, he pitched his own tent (which he had purchased) in such a way that the lines crossed those of his father's tent, which symbolized a united household.

'Ali's household is typical of the majority of Āl Murrah households. Sons continue to live in the household of their father and bring their wives to live with them there. Daughters marry and move out. When a marriage is broken through divorce or death and remarriage takes place, certain variations from this basic pattern occur. Sons almost never reside in a tent in which the senior woman is not their mother. An example is provided by the family of the amir of the Āl Murrah who divorced and remarried several times. His first wife continues to live in her tent, one of the two largest of the tribe, while the amir lives with his latest wife in a smaller tent that is usually pitched less than a hundred yards away. The eldest son of the amir and his first wife lives in his mother's tent, along with his wife, their young son, and his unmarried full sisters. A half brother, whose mother (the amir's second wife) died in childbirth, also lives in this tent rather than with his father and his father's new wife. The amir's third wife, whom he also divorced, lives alone in her own tent with two young sons. If a divorced or widowed woman remarries, her sons quickly attempt to establish independent households when they marry. The majority of households, however, are what anthropologists describe as patrilocal—sons bring their wives to live with them in their father's household. Neolocal or new households are established only when the son's mother and father have each remarried. Matrilocal residence—in the household of the mother—occurs only in a few cases when a divorced or widowed mother does not remarry and her sons bring their wives to live with them in her household.

The household in Āl Murrah culture and society is especially associated with three aspects of their life—hospitality, herding, and the special domain of Āl Murrah women. Generous hospitality is one of the strongest of Āl Murrah values. The greatest praise they bestow on a person is to say that he is a man who is generous and who kills an animal—whatever he has—for his guests. A guest is a sacred trust and is highly honored, even if he is from an enemy group. Hospitality among the Āl Murrah is dispensed equally from all their households. In this regard they differ from some of the bigger Bedouin tribes of the Syrian Desert among whom hospitality is centered around the shaikhs of the tribe. These shaikhs entertain guests on a lavish scale and a stranger would normally direct himself to the tent of the shaikh rather than to that of an ordinary tribesman, although tradition requires that even a poor tribesman in these tribes receive and grant unquestioning hospitality to a guest.

The Āl Murrah contrast themselves with the Shammar, among whom they say can only drink coffee in the tent of the shaikh. Every tent of the Āl Murrah, they say, has its own coffee pots and in every tent you will find the same generous hospitality (although the Āl Murrah shaikhs are also lavishly hospitable). My Āl Murrah companions were shocked at the behavior of the amir of the Subai' tribe when we paid a call on him near a small town in northeast Arabia. He offered us only coffee and tea and did not offer us a meal. When we left, they deemed him a little man. Whenever we visited any of the shaikhs of the Āl Murrah, we were always feted with huge meals which included a sheep slaughtered in our honor. We received the same generosity from every other Āl Murrah tent we visited, but I always refused to allow them to sacrifice an animal unless it was a special occasion that I could reciprocate.

Rashid ibn Talib, the eldest son of the amir of the Āl Murrah, once made a short trip to Iran. On the road between Shiraz and Isphahan, he saw some black tents of Iranian nomads and he wanted to meet them. He stopped and went over to them with an interpreter. He was fascinated to see these nomads of a different cultural and linguistic background, but he was struck by their lack of hospitality. He said they asked him straight away what his business was and did not even offer him tea. When he told me of this encounter, he and I reasoned that this must reflect the patterns of stratification of most of the Iranian tribes where the leaders are very powerful and there is a great deal of differentiation between the lifestyles of the leaders and the common tribespeople. The same distinction holds for the bigger and less dispersed Bedouin tribes of the Syrian Desert where the shaikhs dominate tribal life more than they do among the Āl Murrah. That Āl Murrah households are equal in their dispensation of hospitality symbolizes the basic autonomy and independence of the household in Āl Murrah culture and society—which is itself a consequence of their ecological adaptation as camel nomads.

The coffee ceremony, which takes place in the men's section of the tent, is a central feature of Āl Murrah hospitality—and indeed an essential part of their ritual life. The Āl Murrah drink weak coffee throughout the day, but it takes on special importance whenever a guest arrives. Although a pot of coffee may already be prepared when a guest arrives, a fresh pot is always prepared. The youngest male adult takes charge. He has extra fuel put on the fire in front of the men's section of the tent and then calls out to the women to give him some water and some coffee beans. These are brought and handed to him over the tent divider without the women being seen. The water is put on the fire to boil in a large blackened pot; the beans are roasted to a very light brown in a long-handled skillet and then dumped into a heavy brass mortar. When they have cooled a bit, the man beats them with a brass pestle, hitting the side of the mortar in such a way that it rings out—an invitation to whoever hears it to come and drink coffee. When the beans have been crushed into powder, they are dumped into a shiny brass long-beaked coffee pot. Boiling water is poured into this pot which is set on the fire to come to a boil again. The man now calls out to the women to give him some cardamom. A small handful of cardamom beans are handed over and these are crushed in the mortar and dumped into the pot, which is once again put on the fire and brought to a boil. A plate of dates is handed over from the women's section and these are passed around—first to the guest and then to all the others according to age. The man who made the coffee takes five or six small cups stacked one on top of the other in his right hand. He holds the pot in his left hand and pours a few drops in a cup. He drinks some of it and pours the rest on the ground. Then he moves to where the guest is sitting in the center of a semicircle behind the fire and pours him about a third of a little cup of coffee. He proceeds around the semicircle until all the cups are used. He goes back and begins refilling the cups until the person indicates that he has had enough or tells him to take his cup and continues serving the other people present. Only after a guest has drunk coffee does he state his business, if he has any. Although tea does not figure in the traditional ritual and a guest is free to leave after he has drunk coffee, nowadays tea usually follows the first pot of coffee. Then one drinks one more cup of coffee—"to take away the taste of the tea." Incense is often passed around, too.

The second aspect of Āl Murrah society and culture with which the household is especially associated is herding. It is the main production and consumption unit in their economy—and what little exchange they engage in occurs between members of the household and the wider extra-tribal society through the medium of urban-based markets. As already shown in chapter two, descent groups other than the household figure in the organization of Āl Murrah herding. Major water wells and agricultural plots are most commonly associated with the lineage, and in most summer camps, the residents are members of a single lineage. Most of the members of a lineage graze the same pasture areas during the fall, winter, and spring seasons, but there is no authority other than custom that compels them to so do. Lineage solidarity and exclusivity is seldom absolute. Although one is influenced by the lineage and by concern for one's relatives through marriage, each household provides for its own subsistence and is alone respon- sible for the management of its herd.

Each household has its own herd. Many herds include a few animals that are privately owned by individuals who are not members of the household, but their products are for the use of the herders. Individual members of the household sometimes own a few of the herd's animals as their own private property, but most of the animals of any herd are held communally by the group as a whole. Most are inherited from the paternal grand- father of the group, although some come as part of the dowry or inheritance of women who have married into the household. This core of the herd is held in trust, so to speak, by the senior male of the household for all its members. He cannot sell or give away any of these animals without the consent of the other mem- bers of the household; the division of a herd signifies the division of the household itself.

The third way in which the household figures prominently in Āl Murrah culture and society is as the special domain of women. Although most marriages are within the lineage, the household is the unit into and out of which marriages are contracted. Women leave the households in which they were born and move to that in which their husband resides. In this system, the men stay put and only move into a new household following the division of the herd—usually, though not always, subsequent to the death of their father. Thus it might appear that men are the core members of a household. The reality of Āl Murrah family life, however, coupled with their ideology, suggests that women are the real core of this most basic unit of Āl Murrah society. The tent belongs to the women, as already mentioned. Beyond its confines, men and considerations of patrilineality gain in importance, but within the household itself the women are certainly more than mere outsiders who happen to have married in.

Hassan Fathy, an architect, has described, though with reference to sedentary people, this central aspect of the Arab household:

The inward-looking Arab house, open to the calm of the sky, made beautiful by the feminine element of water, self-contained and peaceful, the deliberate antithesis of the harsh public world of work, warfare, and commerce, is the domain of woman. The name in Arabic "sakan," to denote the house, is related to the word "sakina," peaceful and holy, while the word "harim" which means woman is related to "harem," sacred, which denotes the family living quarters in the Arab house. [Fathy 1969: 77–78]

The same distinction holds true for the Āl Murrah. Women—the mere presence of women—constitutes the essence of the household. The men are always coming and going, often spending nights away from their households while they are herding, on a hunting trip, or on business in the city. The women almost always remain at home in their tents in the desert, even if their husbands are permanently employed in the city. Indeed, for a wife to reside permanently with her husband in the city signifies their break from tribal society. So long as the wife remains in her tent with the herd, the husband remains a member of the tribe, though he may spend long years away.

MARRIAGE AND DIVORCE

After camels, their abiding passion, the next most popular topic of conversation among the Āl Murrah is marriage and divorce. Whenever a traveler returns to his tent, the women almost immediately ask him for news of divorces, marriages, and births—usually in that order. Marriages and divorces, which both involve prolonged periods of negotiation and discussion, are the most important social events among the Āl Murrah. Marriages, as among most nonindustralized people, involve not only the man and woman in a special relationship but their kinspeople as well. When a marriage occurs, a series of bonds is established between the families of the bride and of the groom, and most of the conflicts that arise and cause divorces stem from interfamily problems rather than personal problems between the man and woman.

The Āl Murrah most often marry within a very small circle of kinspeople. As throughout the Middle East, they express a strong preference for marriage between a man and his *bint 'amm*, his paternal uncle's daughter. After his sister, his first cousin on the paternal side is his closest patrilineal relative of the same generation. That he is marrying a woman from within his own descent group rather than someone from outside his descent group, as is common in most societies which proscribe cousin marriages, raises an interesting question of anthropological theory. The theory holds that one accomplishment of marriage in small-scale, kinship-oriented societies is the alliance of disparate descent groups. Since the bride's and groom's families are already closely related to each other through shared descent from a common ancestor, does marriage play any important alliance role in Middle Eastern societies?

This is not the place to review all the anthropological literature on patrilateral parallel cousin marriage in the Middle East, but we should note that the Āl Murrah do not always marry their *bint 'amm*. They also have a high degree of marriages with women who are not their immediate first cousins but who are members of the same lineage. To a much less degree, they also marry women from other lineages and clans. Men from the families of chiefs occasionally marry women from other tribes, and a few of the women of these families marry up into the royal families of Saudi Arabia and the states of the Arabian Gulf. The Āl Murrah never allow any of their women to marry down into any group that is of lower social status. Men may marry women of lower status, but their offspring are not considered to be full members of the tribe, and intermarriage of these with Āl Murrah women is forbidden. As long as any marriage is contracted between parties of equal status, even from different tribes, they are considered *helal,* virtuous, by the Āl Murrah. They prefer, nonetheless, that a man marry a woman who is a close relative.

The major reason the Āl Murrah give for preferring marriages between closely related persons is that these marriages are more likely to be successful and not to result in divorce. The bride, they say, is much happier marrying into a family that she already knows and that is likely to remain close to her own during the course of migrations and summer camp. A bride who goes off to live with a man from another lineage, clan, or tribe will miss her relatives, who will not be nearby to protect her. This potential problem is mitigated somewhat in those few cases in which families from different descent groups have traditions of intermarriage over several generations, although the patterns of migrations and summer camps are likely to keep them separated for long periods of time. The important result of marrying close relatives is a potential for less conflict between the new bride and her in-laws into whose house she moves. The bride's mother-in-law may likely be her mother's sister, who—as mother's sister—already has an especially close and affectionate relationship with the bride.

Although we cannot enter into a full-scale discussion of the implications of Āl Murrah marriage practices for an understanding of Middle Eastern marriage systems in general, we should emphasize that the major requirement the Āl Murrah make regarding marriage is not that it join paternal first cousins but that it join equals (except for women who are allowed to marry up into royal families). Their insistence on marriage between persons of equal status suggests, in my opinion, a caste-like society where integration is achieved more through the economic interdependence of different groups of specialists than through marriage. How the Āl Murrah and other Saudi Arabian pastoral tribesmen fit into such a scheme on a society-wide basis is discussed further in chapter 5.

Although alliance is perhaps not the major function of marriage among the Āl Murrah, it still brings different units, usually households, into close cooperation; in some instances, marriage ties supercede those based on common descent. The Āl Murrah say that a man should always attempt to mediate in a conflict between his blood kinsmen and his in-laws and that he should speak out for his in-laws among his blood kinsmen, although in any show-down he is expected to fight with his blood relatives. The most affectionate relationships between generations are those between young people and their mother's brothers and sisters, who according to the Āl Murrah notions of patrilineality, are not blood kins-people but relatives through marriage. As we saw in chapter 2, marriage also affects the structure of camps during seasonal migrations, as in-laws attempt to camp together.

The initiation of marriage negotiations is almost never begun by either the prospective bride or groom. In most cases involving the marriage of first cousins, the decisions have been reached by the fathers of the bride and groom when they were still quite young. When the boy has grown a full beard, usually between eighteen and twenty years old, and the girl is about eighteen, the father of the boy speaks with his brother and a time for the wedding is set. When no *bint 'amm* is available, the father of the boy (or one of his elder brothers) begins to think about his marriage and considers who have suitable daughters. He first approaches families with whom his family has intermarried in past generations. If no one is found among members of his lineage or from among those families from other descent groups with whom he is related through previous marriages, chances are that the marriage of the young man will be delayed for a number of years until a suitable bride from within their group is found. Only if the boy himself happens to know some outside families will his family approach any of these about a marriage, but that situation is unlikely.

Negotiations for marriage are conducted without any fanfare and often drag on for a year or two. The father of the boy casually mentions the subject to the girl's father. He later mentions it to his wife, and if they both agree, the marriage is ready to be planned. The boy's father and the girl's father agree upon how much bride-wealth should be given to the family of the girl. This is usually symbolic between first cousins and may consist of little or no actual transfer of goods or wealth. Noncousin marriages involve transfers of approximately 1,000 riyals ($222 in 1968–70) to the bride's family, most of which they spend on a dowry of household items which the bride takes to her new home. After the marriage has been agreed upon and the bridewealth and dowry have been assembled, the groom and a representative of the bride, usually her brother, go to a religious official in the city and state their desire to marry. The religious official inquires about the blood relationship between them, to assure that the marriage will not be incestuous, and inquires about the consent of the bride to the marriage. If all is in order, he grants his approval and the marriage is registered.

Sometime later the marriage feast is held at the household of the bride. All of the bride's and groom's male relatives sit on carpets in the east end of the tent to drink coffee and tea and savor incense and then eat a young camel sacrificed for the event. Female relatives gather in the women's section and quietly celebrate among themselves. Occasionally, some of the men dance and shoot their guns in the air; this is uncommon among the Āl Murrah although they claim that they love this kind of revelry. At some time during the feasting, the groom leaves the men's section of the tent and goes to a place in the women's section that has been specially prepared for the wedding night, and *ydhakhil,* he goes in, to his bride. Virginity for a new bride is a *sine qua non,* but the Āl Murrah require no blood-stained sheets as proof of virginity, a practice in some Middle Eastern and Mediterranean peasant communities. Indeed, when I told them of this practice, they thought it barbaric. After a few days, the bride moves to her husband's household and resides there until she is to give birth to her first child (almost always within the first year of marriage), at which time she returns to her parents' household to give birth there under her mother's direction.

The wedding festivities of the Āl Murrah contrast sharply with those of most urban and peasant Saudi Arabians and with many other nomadic pastoralists, where larger concentrations of people are common. Weddings among the sedentary population always involve a great deal of revelry—poetry contests, rhythmic beating of drums, and dancing. Āl Murrah celebrations are small affairs, with only a few relatives and an occasional guest in attendance. The wedding and the negotiations preceding it are done in a very casual manner. This does not mean that marriage is not taken seriously; rather that among close kinspeople, used to years of solitary existence in the most isolated regions of Arabia, there is little impetus for fanfare.

Although husbands and wives often develop close personal ties, these are neither consciously encouraged nor publicly displayed except by old couples within the confines of their household. The coldness and indifference with which a husband greets his wife after a period of absence stands in sharp contrast to the warmth and concern he lavishes on his mother, his father's and mother's sisters, and his own sisters. The Āl Murrah recognize love as a strong emotion inherent in both males and females, but proper marriages, they say, are not based on love. Indeed, if a couple is known to be in love, the girl's father will forbid their marriage in fear that his daughter's reputation might be placed in doubt.

Correspondingly, the Āl Murrah never attribute divorce to the incompatibility of the individuals involved. The major factors that contribute to divorce are the problems of living together in a joint household, especially conflicts between mother-in-law and daughter-in-law and between the wife's people and the husband's people. Less often, a man divorces an old wife in order to marry a younger woman, although the Āl Murrah consider this risqué and slightly undesirable.

The frequency of divorce is high. Four out of nine of the old men of the Āl Kurbi minimal lineage among whom I lived had divorced at least once, three of them having divorced three different wives. Two out of eight of the mid-thirties generation had already divorced. Of the seventeen married men of the Āl Kurbi, six (35 percent) had divorced at least once.

Divorce is a male prerogative, for which the husband forfeits the bridewealth he gave to the bride's family at marriage. The woman returns to her natal household with her dowry and any possessions she has acquired during the marriage. Divorce, like marriage, usually involves an extended period of negotiation that drags on over many months or even years before a final settlement occurs. A man must divorce his wife before witnesses three times before their marriage is finally terminated. The normal pattern is for a man to divorce his wife once and for her to return to her natal household. Then, after a few months separation, a reconciliation is arranged, the man presents a gift of gold to the woman, and she returns to his household. A second divorce and reconciliation may follow, even after several years. A third divorce results in a final break, after which the woman is free to remarry. All three divorces can be pronounced in quick succession, but most involve considerable family negotiation over long periods.

A woman does not have the right to initiate divorce proceedings or to force her husband to set her free. She does have the prerogative, however, to leave him at any time and return to her family.

Her husband cannot compel her to rejoin him, but he can refuse to divorce her, thus denying her the freedom to remarry. Wife-initiated separations usually result from the wife's personal unhappiness in the household rather than from conflicts involving the two families.

PATTERNS OF INTERACTION

Patterns of interaction within the household, and indeed throughout the tribe, are influenced by considerations of age, sex, and genealogical relationship. A degree of separation exists between males and females but this is not nearly as absolute among the Āl Murrah camel nomads as among traditionally sedentary people in Saudi Arabia. Males and females are expected to carry out different tasks, to spend leisure time separately, and to have different outlooks on life, but females are not secluded as they are in village and urban Arabia. They move about freely in their herding and household chores and attend urban markets when in the city.

When male guests arrive at the *bayt,* the women curtail some of their movements outside their part of the tent, depending on their degree of relationship with the visitors, the duration of the visit, and their actual need to leave the tent. When no guests are present, older women pass much of their idle time in the men's section, especially in the early evening, where they participate actively in the conversations. Younger women spend less time in the men's section, although they sometimes sit there when no men are around or at night when they gather around the fire to listen to (and occasionally to participate in) the talk that lasts until around midnight.

How relationship influences interaction is seen in the ritual ways of greeting different kinds of people. Male visitors from among the Āl Murrah themselves first approach the men's section of the tent, where they greet all the men present, one by one. If they are young men up to about thirty and from the same lineage, they kiss each other lightly on the lips. If they are middle-aged or older, or if they come from different lineages, they touch noses two or three times. When an old man is greeted, his younger lineage mates kiss his nose while members of other lineages either kiss his nose or simply touch noses.

After all the men have been greeted, the visitors greet the women of the *bayt*. If they come from other lineages and there are no marital relationships, they simply direct a verbal greeting across the tent divider and do not go in to see them. If they are from the same lineage, however, they go into the women's section of the tent and greet the women directly. If they are from different minimal lineages, they shake hands. If they are from the same minimal lineage, the man lifts the veil of the woman and kisses her on the cheek without regard to age or marital status.

If the visitors are not from among the Āl Murrah, they simply shake hands with the men and do not greet the women at all. If, however, the women know the visitors, they may greet the men verbally from their side of the tent. Any women who arrive with male visitors go directly, and from the back side of the tent, to the women's section. If they are Āl Murrah women, the men of the *bayt* go to them at some time during the visit to greet them.

These differences in greetings reflect differences in more general patterns of interaction. The most informal and affectionate relationship is that between boys and young men from the same lineage. Whenever they are together and not busy herding, they wrestle playfully, run foot races, or talk and joke with each other. As they become older, they adopt a more serious and formal stance, although almost every adult Marri under fifty is always ready to run a foot race or wrestle with a friend or crack a joke. Older males and men from other lineages are treated with deference and respect. Men from other tribes are treated with reserve unless they are known quite well.

Āl Murrah men are expected to treat Āl Murrah women with consideration and respect. In formal situations, they maintain a high degree of reserve, but younger people, when alone or in the company of close relatives, joke and laugh with each other. Both young men and young unmarried women somewhat playfully flirt with each other, although not in the presence of the woman's father or brothers.

Clothing for both sexes is decorous. Āl Murrah women past puberty wear black mask-like veils that cover their entire face, with slits for the eyes. Their bodies are fully covered with long-sleeved dresses that reach to their feet and pantaloons that completely cover their legs. A black head-covering conceals their hair, which is parted in the middle and woven into long braids. Most women, especially younger ones, wear *kohl,* a heavy black cosmetic, around their eyes and sometimes put henna dye on the palms of their hands. They usually wear a number of rings of gold or silver, set with semiprecious stones, on their fingers or on a loop that hangs from their headdress. Thus, women adorn themselves to make themselves more attractive, but they should not appear actively seductive.

Men likewise keep their bodies fully clothed and their heads covered. They never undress completely except when taking private showers in public baths in the oil company barracks. When bathing themselves at wells in the desert, they keep on at least their underwear even in all-male company. They do not wear veils, although their headdress is often concealingly wrapped around the face for protection. No jewelry is worn except for an occasional signet ring. *Kohl* is sometimes worn around the eyes but the men say it is for medicinal purposes rather than beauty.

All Āl Murrah men have beards. Long, shoulder-length hair parted in the middle is considered especially becoming and manly and is said to make them more attractive to women. Yemeni-made decorated cartridge belts filled with bullets and silver Omani daggers are worn at least as much for show as for protection, especially by younger males. The men also very much enjoy strong perfumes and incense.

Sex, though seldom discussed openly, is an activity that men, at least, feel that both they and the women should enjoy. I was never able to question any women about their feelings on the subject, but the men invariably expressed a belief that it is only natural for women to enjoy sex, though they feel that a "proper" woman should not express her enjoyment.

Premarital sex is uncommon for males and taboo for females. Men seldom discuss sex among themselves, and I rarely heard them mention it except when someone occasionally asked me about the sex habits of Americans. Unmarried men have few opportunities for sexual encounters. Several of my young friends talked jokingly about an old divorced woman and told me about encountering prostitutes among nomads in Iraq during the course of winter migrations. Male homosexuality is occasionally joked about but to my knowledge is never engaged in by the more isolated nomads such as the Āl 'Azab. Young men who have worked in oil company camps or lived in a major urban area are more aware of homosexuality but have seldom had such relations. Masturbation is considered polluting and not ordinarily practiced. Some unmarried young men admit to having nocturnal emissions which they attribute to *jinns* which have visited them in the night.

Opportunity for sex is often described as one of the greatest pleasures of marriage. Because of close quarters and lack of privacy, married couples perform intercourse at night with a minimum of precoital love play, without undressing, and with practically no sounds. A man ejaculates quickly, sometimes within a minute of insertion. He occasionally continues coitus until he has ejaculated a second or even a third time. The proper sexual position, according to the men, is for the man to enter the woman from behind as she faces away from him; face-to-face coitus is considered risqué.

Except for sleeping together at night, men and women actually spend very little time together. They eat separately and have few common tasks. There is a clear sexual division of labor, but both sexes perform activities mainly associated with the other sex under certain conditions. For example, women cook all meals consumed at home in their tent, although men traveling away from the herds cook their own food even when accompanied by women. Women are concerned with taking down, setting up, and transporting all household items, including the tent, but any men who are not busy will help them, especially in loading the heavier items. Men are mainly concerned with herding, milking, and watering camels, but women perform any of these tasks. Men do not know how to weave, but they do knit socks and gloves for their own use during winter and udder protectors for their camels in milk. Women do not drive automobiles but neither do many of the men. Both men and women attend markets and buy and sell products. Men alone hunt and slaughter and skin all animals for feasting and serve meals to their guests. Women are the only ones who assist others in giving birth. Thus most household and herding activities are parceled out according to sex but are shared when there is a shortage of hands. Both men and women are more or less equally burdened; both are busy and active all day long.

In spite of the separation between the sexes, there are also strong feelings of unity. The women and the men equally feel themselves members of the tribe, clan, and lineage, and they are proud of these affiliations. The women perhaps express a greater concern for purity than the men, whom they berate for allowing themselves to come into contact with foreigners and people whom they consider to be less pure Arabs.

Men express the highest regard for their mothers and sisters although they often seem to slight their wives. Sons always mention their concern for their mothers and her sisters and brothers, and they make special efforts to visit them if the families are separated and to look after their mothers if they have been divorced. In spite of men's hesitation to express any affection for their wives, many husbands and wives clearly develop very close ties and live together for years of happy marriage based on intimate communication and concern for each other.

A definite description of patterns of interaction within the household and an evaluation of differences between the sexes is difficult, at best, because of the subtleties and nuances of feelings that are a part of all personal relationships. Where separation of the sexes and generations occurs, the problems become even more difficult, since the investigator will probably be denied access to one or more of the categories of people concerned. As a male ethnographer, I could not come to know any of the Āl Murrah women as well as I came to know the men, and the point of view I express is based primarily on my understanding derived from men. A more complete understanding of household structure and family life must necessarily await a male-female team that can sit and talk on both sides of the tent.

Any situation involving separation may provide a basis for inequality. The separation of the sexes begins at an early age among the Āl Murrah, but because of the requirements of their nomadic way of life, it never becomes as absolute as it does among sedentary Arabs. Boys as young as three years are allowed to spend most of the day in the men's section of the tent where they are taught war cries and are given little knives to carry around like daggers. Girls at this age spend some time among the men, but as they grow older they spend most of their time among the women. As the boys grow older, the men begin to teach them the genealogy of their closer relations and encourage them to help in making coffee and dispensing hospitality. By the time they are five, they are taken herding, and by the time they are seven or eight they begin actively to help with the herds. By the time the girls are five they no longer visit the men's section of the tent and spend all their time with the women.

There is no denying that women take second place in many situations. Men eat and drink coffee before the women, although a man sometimes defers drinking a cup of coffee until after his mother has had some. Men lead a decidedly more varied life outside the household and have many more opportunities for socializing than do the women. But it would be hard to characterize their relationship as one of exploitation or of gross inequality because nomadic pastoralism requires the coordination of household and herding activities and depends on the active cooperation of all members of the family unit, male and female, young and old.

Finally, the ideology of the Āl Murrah kinship system stresses the unity of all its members. Although descent is calculated through males from a male ancestor, membership in the tribe includes both sexes and depends on being born of an Āl Murrah woman. Āl Murrah women are full members of the group, and are respected as such. Since most marriages are contracted within the tribe, marriage brings in few outsiders. Although divorce is relatively common, it results more often from conflict between the wife and her mother-in-law than from conflict with her husband. Aside from the mother-in-law problem, conflict between the generations is essentially unknown among the Āl Murrah. A high degree of easygoing respect characterizes most relationships between the young and the old. Both are equally engrossed in their camels and in the social and political events at all levels of the tribe. As some of the young begin to go to work in cities and to change some of their traditional ideas, conflict may develop. As yet, however, the unity of tribal affiliation and the common concern of pastoralism overrides any serious conflicts between young and old or between males and females.

Merzuq, a skilled hunter, sits with his rifle
to which he has attached a shoulder padding made
of the dried skins of the faces of gazelles
he has killed. The cartridge belt he wears was
made by Yemeni craftsmen.

Characteristic physical features of the
Rub' al Khali. The bush in the foreground is
called abal and stays green for four years after a
single rain. Clumps of tall grass grow in the
sandy areas between sand dunes.

An old man recites a
poem about camels before
departing from a coffee
session in the men's
section of the tent.

A man practices his shooting while mounted on
an Omani thoroughbred riding camel.

A youth departs in the morning from his parent's tent to go to his herd where he will spend the rest of the day. He carries a rifle and wears a cartridge belt for protection, although no raids have occurred for decades. His younger brother poses with another rifle and looks forward to when he will be old enough to start herding.

Men, old and young, sit and drink coffee in the afternoon and discuss the state of pasturage while they are migrating during the winter in northeastern Arabia. Young boys join the men while their sisters remain with their mothers in another part of the tent. In the background is the ru'ag, the divider woven by the women to separate the men's section of the tent from that of the women.

*Typical landscapes in the Rub' al-Khali,
a 200,000 square mile expanse of desert in
southeastern Arabia. It has no permanent
settlements but is the homeland of the Āl Murrah
Bedouin and of several smaller tribes.*

*Two old men and two boys sit on the top
of a sand dune in the Rub' al-Khali. One of the
men has a pair of binoculars to better
observe his camels.*

A thoroughbred milk camel, from the ash-Shuruf
breed, pauses at an abal bush in the Rub' al-Khali.
The halter-like apparatus she wears helps keep
a woolen protector in place over her udder to
prevent her offspring from suckling.

Al-Kurbi, the author's guide, pours freshly
brewed coffee to his mother's brother's son and
his half brother (through the mother) while on a
hunting trip in the Rub' al-Khali. Coffee beans
and cardamon seeds are carried in the
leather bags in the foreground.

In late fall, camels begin to migrate to pastures in
the north where rains have fallen.

The author's riding camel, a thoroughbred
Omani, grazes leaves from an abal bush. The
saddle was purchased by the Bedouin in Hofuf.
The saddle bags were woven by the
women of the tribe.

Two salugi hunting dogs, relatives of greyhounds, rest by a desert bush. Every tent of the Āl Murrah has at least one such dog. They catch hares and some are even said to catch and kill gazelles.

Two brothers water their father's camels at a well in the northern part of the Rub' al-Khali. Their bucket and their trough are made of leather.

The author stands in front of two male baggage camels which have just been watered at a well in the Rub' al-Khali.

The Āl Murrah especially value water that collects in shallow ponds after a winter rain. Here, two youths fill big rubber innertubes to take back to their tent for household use.

Al-Kurbi, the author's guide, offers a bowl of milk to his father's brother while his father, older brother, son and his brother's son look on. The brass pots in the foreground are coffee pots.

The days and nights are cold during the winter and these men wear a variety of traditional cloaks, Western-style jackets, and—second from left—a heavy sheepskin coat.

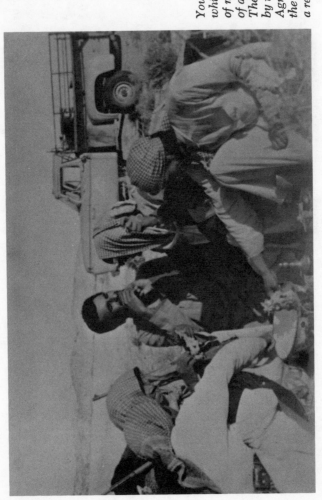

Young men laugh and joke while eating a breakfast of pieces of meat left over from the slaughter of a sheep the night before. The author's truck, loaned him by the Saudi Arabian Ministry of Agriculture and Water, is typical of the vehicles that are becoming a regular feature of desert Arabia.

A man pauses in front of the tent with his tan riding camel before departing.

Chapter 4

SEGMENTATION AND THE LINEAGE, CLAN, AND TRIBE

The rhythm of nomadism in the deserts of Arabia is determined by seasonal variation and the vagaries of rainfall. The desert situation demands mobility and requires that individual households be able to move separately during certain seasons and then to come together in larger units at other times. Access to water and to pastures must be regulated. The social structural mechanism adapted to these requirements is what is commonly referred to by anthropologists as the segmentary lineage system. This is a pervasive type of social structure that is widely found among nomadic pastoralists throughout the desert areas of the Middle East. In this system, every household unites according to the principles of patrilineal descent to form segments that are more and more inclusive of kinsmen. Among the Āl Murrah, the lineage, which includes all the people descended from a male ancestor who existed about five generations ago, averages approximately fifty households each. Clans group together from four to six lineages, and the Āl Murrah tribe is composed of seven clans.

This system encompasses both groups and patterns of group process. Every person, male and female, is a member of a number of different groups—household, lineage, clan, and tribe—each one of which bears the name of a male ancestor and each one of which includes increasingly more people. But we cannot focus exclusively on the composition and role of each level of grouping. We must pay equal attention to the process of segmentation itself, since it not only brings more and more groups into relationship with each other but, when coupled with their kinship terminology system, allows people to relate to each other as close relatives, even when genealogically they are far removed. It is perhaps the fluidity of this system that is most characteristic. Named groups exist and people readily identify themselves as members of them, but the nomadic rhythm constantly brings people into contact with others from different groups to whom there must be ways of relating. Similarly, while the named kin groups persist through time, the actual group that effectively operates together varies widely from season to season, and the amalgamations of one year seldom exactly repeat themselves the next.

Before giving some concrete examples of how this system works in everyday situations, we must briefly look at the kinship terminology system of the Āl Murrah, since this reflects how they conceive of their kinspeople and is an integral part of their relations with them. Actually, the Āl Murrah have two terminology systems. One is highly descriptive of specific individuals: different terms are used to refer to father, mother, brother, sister, father's brother, mother's brother, father's sister, mother's sister, father's brother's/ sister's daughter/son; mother's brother's/sister's daughter/son, son, daughter, grandfather, and grandmother. This system allows a person to single out a specific kinsperson and precisely state what relationship exists.

The other system is extensive, or classificatory, and allows a person to include large numbers of people into close relationship with him even when close genealogical relationships do not exist. Thus all members of one's own generation are addressed as brother or sister; all members of one's mother's and father's generation and above are addressed as mother or father; and all members of one's children's generation or below are addressed as son or daughter. The terms for grandfather and grandmother are extended to include all ancestors, no matter how far removed. The term for father's brother (and consequently father's brother's son/daughter) is commonly extended to refer not only to one's actual father's brother but to any distant relative whose ancestor was the brother of one's ancestor any number of generations ago.

Often while I was traveling in the desert with al-Kurbi we would spot a herd of camels and a herder. We would drive over to the herder and greet him. By looking at the brand on the camels, al-Kurbi would immediately know whether they were from the Āl Murrah and, in most cases, from what lineage. By listening to the man's speech he could also tell if he were from the Āl Murrah or some other tribe. If he were indeed from the Āl Murrah, he would always address the man as son of my father's brother, *ibn 'ammi*, even though he had never seen the man before and their closest common ancestor lived, say, ten generations ago. To know that he was from the Āl Murrah was to know that he was a member of one's family, a brother, and to know from what lineage he came was to know almost everything about him—where he camps during the summer, who his close relatives are, for what deeds his ancestors are famous, and in what legal and political conflicts he is involved, if any. When the Āl Murrah see an individual they do not know, they ask "What is that?" rather than "Who is that?" To know what group a person comes from immediately places him into perspective regarding the social, political, and spatial organizations of Arabia. If strangers are members of the same tribe, they will address each other as if they were members of the same immediate family, no matter how many generations separate them.

The extension of basic kin terms to more distantly related people occurs under somewhat different circumstances among the sedentary Arabs, but seldom to the degree it occurs among the nomads. Once I traveled with an old man of the Āl Murrah to Riyadh where we visited one of the princes of the Āl Sa'ud; the old man was accompanied by a boy in his teens. The prince asked the old man who the boy was, and the old man replied that the boy was his brother. The prince protested that there was such a difference in their ages and wondered how they could actually be brothers. The old man countered that he was his father's brother's son. The prince still refused to believe him. Finally, the old man admitted that the boy was just a member of the tribe and was not from either his lineage or his clan. To the old man and the boy, however, what was most important in this situation was not that they were in fact distant kinsmen but that they were both from the same tribe and thus brothers.

Descent is traced through males for both men and women. A man is the son of his father, his father's father, and so on. Similarly, a woman is known as the daughter of her father, and so on through the male line. The role of women in birth is recognized by the Āl Murrah, and children of the same mother—though not necessarily of the same father—are grouped together as *ayal al-batn,* children of the womb. Also, children who have suckled from the same woman are related to each other in the same way as those who are related through blood as well. But groups of siblings that are related only through the mother concern only the immediate individuals involved and do not give rise to groups that are of structural importance to the tribe as a whole. Let us turn now to take a closer look at the patrilineal descent groups—the lineage, the clan, and the tribe—which provide the institutional framework of Āl Murrah social, economic, and political life.

THE LINEAGE

The lineage is composed of all the people who are descended from an ancestor who stands about five generations removed from the present adult generations. Most of the lineages of the Āl Murrah group together about fifty households, although some are slightly larger or smaller. The lineage among the Āl Murrah is called a *fakhd,* or thigh, because they are, as they say, the units on which the whole tribe stands. They contrast the *fakhd* with the *'aynin,* the eyes, who are the tribal leaders, who are supposed to look after the interests of the tribe.

The imagery of the *fakhd* as a group which stands together is drawn from a military context. In the days of tribal warfare before the unification of Saudi Arabia under the leadership of the Āl Sa'ud, the *fakhd* fought together under the leadership of an *agid,* a man chosen from within the *fakhd* for his skill and bravery as a warrior. Although tribal wars are now a thing of past, the *fakhd* continues to be an important unit in the military activities of many of the Āl Murrah. Most of the tribes in Saudi Arabia have been incorporated into the National Guard, and in at least the unit in which the Āl Murrah predominate, the lineage continues to be the basis for most subdivisions. However, before the establishment of a centralized state and the creation of a national military structure, the *fakhd* was first of all a defense unit in which all the descendants of a common ancestor fought together to defend themselves and their resources from encroachment by other tribes. Each *fakhd* has its own war cry, which includes the name of a famous camel and the name of a sister in honor of whom one always fights. Within the *fakhd* blood responsibility is equally shared. If a member of the *fakhd* kills an outsider, the whole *fakhd* is responsible for his actions and any male of the group may be killed in retribution or, alternatively, all members contribute equally to paying the *diya,* blood money, to the avenging group. Similarly, if any of its own members are killed, the whole group seeks revenge.

Although the Āl Murrah speak of the lineage in militaristic terms, it is not related only to military activities. How it functions as an economic unit has already been described in chapter two with regard to herding practices. The ownership of wells, one of the most basic resources, is vested in the lineage. As a result, the lineage forms the basis for the composition of most summer camps. In many cases, the lineage founders are credited with having dug the wells or of having taken them from other groups. Nowadays, when wells are redug or are modernized, the members of the lineage cooperate, either as a work group or to hire others to do the work for them. Actual use of the wells by members of the lineage varies slightly from year to year. In most cases, the majority of the members camp together at their wells during the summer, but circumstances sometimes intervene to keep the lineage dispersed even during the summer. For example, the Āl 'Azab were unable to use their well, Bir Fadhil, during the summers of 1969 and 1970 because of modernization works there. During those years they camped not too far away at three smaller wells, with subdivisions of the lineages tending to cling together at each well. Most summer camps also include a few members of other lineages who use the wells as the guests of the owners.

While there is general agreement within the tribe about the ownership of all the major wells within Āl Murrah territories, there are disputes about some of the smaller ones which are used less frequently. Most of the conflicts which occur among the Āl Murrah are between lineages over these wells. An example is a conflict which developed between the Āl 'Azab lineage and the Āl Uwair lineage, both of which are from different clans. The well in question, al-Gasab, is a small well in the north central part of the Rub' al-Khali. No one had used it for numerous years when the Āl Uwair decided to dig it out and cement the upper portion of it. They proceeded to do this and drew their *wasm,* brand, in the cement. When the Āl 'Azab heard of this, a delegation of six older men rode over to the well and informed the Āl Uwair that this well belonged to the Āl 'Azab and that the Āl Uwair had no right to use it without first asking the permission of the Āl 'Azab. They demanded that the Āl Uwair leave the well and remove their brand from the cement. The Āl Uwair refused, and while tempers became very strained, it was agreed to take the case to the amir of al-Hasa for mediation. Each group brought witnesses to claim that they had used the well in the past and that they had the right to it. The Āl 'Azab proved that they had the most ancient claim to the well, showing that they had used it in the summer before 'Abd al-Aziz ibn Sa'ud conquered al-Hasa from the Turks, i.e., in 1912. The amir ruled that the Āl Uwair could stay there since they had brought the well back into use but recognized that the Āl 'Azab also had rights to the well and could use it if they so desired. While this was a peaceful confrontation, settled through litigation, conflicts over wells often lead to violence.

While the lineage is most obvious as a unit of social organization during summer camps, it also plays an important role in organizing migrations during other seasons. Although they do not migrate together as a group, most of the members of a given lineage go to the same general area during each season. When households decide to go to other areas, the rest of the lineage usually knows approximately where they are and is keenly interested in any news about them. As we showed in chapters 2 and 3, the household continues to act as an independent unit, but the lineage tends to cling together whenever possible. Herds are owned by individual households, but all of the animals of the lineage are marked with a single brand and are conceived of as the communal property of the lineage, although each household head has the right to dispose of his animals in any way he chooses. Each lineage also has a distinctive way of calling out or talking to its camels while they are being herded.

Members of the same lineage feel close to each other and think of themselves as one people. Aside from the individual household, the lineage is the only unit of the Āl Murrah that regularly comes together as a single group. The tribe itself never unites as a single group, except potentially in the case of warfare.

Clans rarely unite as an effective social unit. Lineages remain spatially separated from each other, even in the oasis of Jabrin which is occupied every summer by all the lineages of the Āl Jaber clan. Thus the lineage is a very basic unit of Āl Murrah social organization, but it should be remembered that each household is an independent unit and that the relationships between households which unite in a lineage are strictly based on egalitarianism. There are no lineage leaders, except for the *agid* who served as a temporary leader during warfare. There are also no special lineage councils; all decisions are based on consensus.

Although members of a lineage claim that they are all the descendants of an ancestor about five generations removed, shared kinship is not the only factor which keeps the lineage together and makes it a basic unit. Ecological factors play an important—perhaps even a determining—role in defining the actual make-up of the unit. The fact that camels have a kind of homing instinct and, in the absence of concerted efforts to keep them in another area, automatically return to the same wells each summer serves to unite all the members of a lineage each summer at its well. Thus the group that regularly camps together each summer comprises all of the effective members of a lineage. Outsiders, if they regularly camp at the well of another lineage, in time become thought of as members of that lineage. Conversely, when a lineage becomes spatially separated, for whatever reasons, and ceases to camp together during the summers, it effectively divides, and two new groups begin to emerge, each of which in time becomes known as a separate lineage.

Examples of outsiders becoming incorporated into another lineage are numerous in most Arab tribes, for adoption is an easy and regular matter. The desire to seek adoption in another group sometimes stems from situations of conflict in which a person flees his own group and takes refuge with another; should he continue to live with them in subsequent years, he will be considered as a member of that group. Sometimes it is related to a desire to become attached to a particularly powerful group. Among the Āl Murrah it often results from marriages between lineages and usually reflects the man's poverty in camels. If a man from one lineage who is poor in camels marries a woman from a second lineage whose family is wealthy in camels, the man will tend to become a member of the woman's lineage and will be treated as if he were a patrilineal descendant of the woman's lineage.

There was one such man who lived and traveled with the Āl 'Azab and was usually called an 'Azabi, although he was formally a member of another lineage.

An example of the divisions that occur in lineages when they become spatially separated is provided by the Āl 'Azab. All of our references to this group, so far, have referred specifically to only 35 out of 51 tents of the Āl 'Azab. These 35 households are the camel herders among whom I lived, all of whom base themselves at Bir Fadhil in the Rub' al-Khali. The rest of the Āl 'Azab have become sheep and goat herders and base themselves at wells in the al-Hasa area, about 400 miles to the north of Bir Fadhil. Neither of these groups ever comes together for any reasons related to herding. They move in completely different circles. Neither group is ever concerned or knowledgeable about the movements of the other, although each group is keenly aware of the movements of its own households. Each group is also in contact with different sets of outside groups. The Āl 'Azab camel herders, for example, have much more contact with the Āl Jaber clan, whose base in Jabrin is not far from their own, than they do with members of other clans that are more closely related to them genealogically. The Āl 'Azab sheep and goat herders associate more with the northern based lineages of the Āl Fuhaidah clan than do the Āl 'Azab camel herders.

The separation of these two groups of the Āl 'Azab is recognized by the rest of the Āl Murrah, who habitually ask about the state of the two gatherings, referring to them as the southerners and the northerners respectively. People from other clans, who do not know the precise genealogical relationships of these people, are beginning to consider the Āl 'Azab camel herders as a separate clan, since it is relatively large and operates with a high degree of isolation from other groups of the Āl Murrah. These people would merge the northern Āl 'Azab with the Āl Fuhaidah clan. In spite of this beginning differentiation as a result of changes in herding practices and the spatial displacement of the two groups, all of the Āl 'Azab continue to think of themselves as a single social unit and blood responsibility is shared equally within the genealogical group. In time, however, they may very well emerge as distinct social groups.

An important feature of Āl Murrah lineages is that they are all relatively equal in size and wealth. There are three lineages— no more than a tenth of the tribe—which are socially tainted and with whom the rest of the Āl Murrah claim one should not inter-marry. Each of these groups is reputed to be descended from a union between an Āl Murrah male and a woman of slave status, and because of this, they are considered impure and of lower status. In the past, these lineages were very poor in camels and many of their members worked as herders for members of other Āl Murrah lineages. Recently, however, the general economic position of these three lineages has improved considerably and they no longer work for other Āl Murrah. Accordingly, their social status seems to be improving, especially in the eyes of younger members of the Āl Murrah who are less interested in genealogical history than are some of their elders. Most of the rest of the Āl Murrah, at least 90 percent of the tribe, are members of lineages that are essentially equal in wealth, power, and social status.

That there is not greater differentiation among Āl Murrah lineages is directly related to ecology. Wells and the pastures around them can only be used within certain limits. The maximum capacity of the Āl Murrah's bigger wells, such as Bir Fadhil, does not exceed 40 to 50 tents. If more households and their herds camp at these places, there would be the danger of exhausting the water supply and especially of overgrazing the areas around the well, factors of which the Āl Murrah are fully conscious. Āl Murrah wells are also highly scattered at great distances from each other. Thus it is impossible for large concentrations to occur for any extended period of time.

The horizontal pattern of Āl Murrah migrations does not require them to cross major natural barriers or into or through foreign or potentially hostile areas that would require large concentrations for protection. They migrate in small units and do not rely on the coordinating activities of any leaders. This is in striking contrast to many nomadic pastoralists who practice vertical nomadism and who migrate as a mass along predetermined paths under the leadership of a powerful chief. Many of the tribes in Iran, for example, stand in marked contrast to the Āl Murrah because of their powerful leaders who play major roles in coordinating mass migrations from one pasture area to another pasture area across nontribally controlled territory. The environment the Āl Murrah operate in does not require highly coordinated herding practices or migrations and the tribal leaders of the Āl Murrah play only a token role in pastoral activities, although they are important in relating the tribe to the outside world.

CLANS

Aside from dividing themselves into households and lineages, the Āl Murrah also divide themselves into seven different clans, each of which includes four to six lineages. The term the Āl Murrah use for this unit is *gabila*, which is usually translated into English as tribe. These units, however, are intermediate between the lineage and the unit which includes all the people descended from Murrah, and to avoid confusion I prefer to call them clans, especially since the Āl Murrah as a whole have a paramount amir and are recognized as a tribal unit by the Saudi Arabian state.

The clans are essentially residual units and play no active role in the economic organization of the Āl Murrah. No major resources such as wells or pastures are specifically vested in them. Yet all the lineages of a clan feel especially close to each other, and when wells are shared between members of different lineages, more likely than not they came from the same clan. The clans are more important as political units. Five of the seven clans of the Āl Murrah have minimal lineages which are considered of special amir status, three of which have provided paramount amirs for the whole tribe. All political actions—to defend one's resources, to gain concessions from the government, to seek vengeance, or to settle legal disputes—involve the support of the clan as a whole and require the participation of the amir of the clan. Although the clan plays little role in organizing migrations and the ownership of herds and wells is formally vested in the lineage, it plays an important role in power relationships, since any individual or any lineage can count on the automatic support of all the lineages of a clan in any conflict.

Clans are critical in the process of segmentation. Political and military coalitions seldom extend beyond the level of the clan, although the segmentary system provides mechanisms for coalitions all the way to the level of the tribe and even beyond. Clans are linked together in pairs by means of a common ancestor who brings them into relationship with another clan, as in figure 4. The relationship of clans to each other is based on the principle

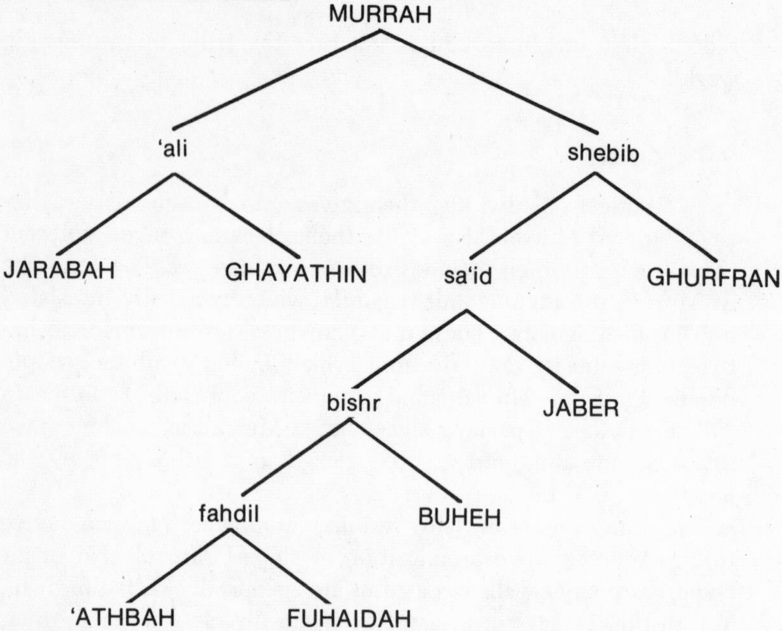

Figure 4. Āl Murrah Clans. The names written in capitals are clans. The other names are of presumed common ancestors serving as connecting links.

of dual opposition and is usually expressed in terms of military action. For example, a man from the Āl Fuhaidah clan says that, given a conflict, the Āl Fuhaidah and the Āl 'Athba join together as the Āl Fadhil to fight against the Āl Buheh, but they join with the Āl Buheh as the Āl Bishr to fight against the Āl Jaber. The Āl Jaber and the Āl Bishr unite as the Āl Sa'id against the Āl Ghurfran, but both of these join as the Āl Shebib against the Āl 'Ali, who are divided into two clans, the Āl Jarabah and the Āl Ghayathin. The Āl Ali and the Āl Shebib unite as the Āl Murrah. The conflict model is not always used in explaining this system, since they sometimes say that Murrah had two sons, 'Ali and Shebib; 'Ali also had two sons, Jarabah and Gayathin; Shebib had two sons, Ghurfran and Sa'id; Sa'id had two sons, Jaber and Bishr; Bishr had two sons, Buheh and Fadhil, and Fadhil had two sons, Fuhaidah and 'Athba.

The way in which clans relate to each other according to dualistic opposition is a function of the segmentary system, which always seeks to bring more and more groups together. Actual coalitions never strictly follow this system. Intervening levels are sometimes skipped, as when, say, the Āl Fuhaidah and the Āl Jaber want to interact, for whatever reasons, they claim that they are the Āl Sa'id, their closest common ancestor, without necessarily implicating all the other groups which also claim Sa'id as an ancestor, although the other groups could very easily be brought into such a coalition simply through an appeal to the duties of all the descendants of a given ancestor to stand together. Such is the process of segmentation.

THE TRIBE

The tribe is the unit which includes all of the descendants, male and female, of Murrah, a personage who is said to have lived before the beginning of Islam. A tradition states that his wife and the progenitress of all his descendants was a *jinnia,* a female spirit. The assertion that they descend from a *jinnia* reflects the position they occupy among other Saudi Arabian tribes. On the one hand, they are fully recognized as a noble tribe, the descendants of Murrah, a free Arab. But they inhabit the Rub' al-Khali, the Empty Quarter, which according to popular Arabian folklore is the abode of *jinns,* and they have uncanny abilities to track people and animals. As a result, they are slightly tainted in the popular eye, although none deny their high status.

The tribe marks a significant social and cultural boundary. Such things as dialect, fashions in clothing and grooming, verbal and nonverbal ways of greeting, and styles in poetry, songs, and weaving are all closely bounded by the tribe. The tribe marks the limit of effective kinship, although the process of segmentation continues past the level of the tribe and brings other tribes into special genealogical relationship with the Āl Murrah. Marriage, which is already highly endogamous at the lineage level, reaches almost 100 percent endogamy at the level of the tribe. Only a few women from the tribe marry out into other tribes or into the royal family to symbolize alliances with these other groups. Loyalty to the tribe and its essential unity is strongly articulated by the Āl Murrah, who frequently repeat, *"Āl Murrah, kuluna wahid; biyutna wahid; kuluna ikhwan"*: "People of Murrah, we are all one; our tents are one; we are all brothers."

Within the complex society of Arabia, the tribe traditionally has been an important political unit. Prior to the concentration of power under the Āl Sa'ud, the tribe was essentially autonomous and wielded a great deal of military strength, providing for its own protection and defense and usually extending military protection to urban areas, peasant villages, and even other nomadic pastoralists, especially sheep herders. All of the major tribes of Arabia have a strong military ethos and think of themselves as warriors as much as herders. Tribal leaders are associated mainly with military activities rather than anything directly related to pastoralism. Today, the tribe no longer enjoys the same degree of autonomy as in the past and tribal leaders base their power on their abilities to act as intermediaries between the members of the tribe and the rulers of Saudi Arabia. Yet the tribe continues to be a primary unit of political identification, and people relate to the state as members of a tribe rather than as individual citizens. No individual, for example, would think of initiating any major action with the state without the permission and collaborative support of his tribal leaders.

Although the tribe stands out as an important military, political, social, and cultural unit, its base is economic. The tribe is the unit which claims a kind of eminent domain, or sovereignty over the central pasture areas used by the tribe. *Dirat-Āl Murrah,* Āl Murrah territories, discussed in chapter two, comprise the core pasture areas of the Āl Murrah. They do not belong to them in the sense of private property, and the tribe is not a corporate group that has any legal title to the land in the modern sense of owning land that can be bought and sold. Āl Murrah territories are lands over which the Āl Murrah have established their control through military conquest and the displacement of other tribes. Other tribes or subunits of other tribes are welcome to pass through and use any of the pastures and wells of this area on a temporary basis. Occasionally small groups of Bedouin from tribes to the south of the Rub' al-Khali migrate into Āl Murrah territories where they are welcomed, so long as they don't attempt to establish themselves permanently. Conversely, the Āl Murrah regularly migrate outside of their own territories to graze lands that are the territories of other tribes. In selecting pasture areas outside their own territories, they have to take into consideration the state of the pastures themselves, the existence of other pastoralists in the same areas, and the existence of peaceful relations with the tribes which claim the areas. At present, peaceful relations exist between the Āl Murrah and the tribes to the north of them into whose territories they migrate during the winter and spring. At times in the past, before the curtailment of tribal wars after the development of the state, their use of these lands was directly related to their military prowess and ability to defend themselves, although the peaceful sharing of wells and pastures on a temporary basis is traditional in the absence of feuds or other major conflicts. Internally, the pastures of the tribal territories are not subdivided and are equally open to all members of the tribe. Only wells and small oases, where they exist, belong to subunits of the tribe, almost always the lineage.

The relationship between the tribe, military prowess, and economics is seen in the ancient custom of raiding, which is now strictly forbidden by the Saudi Arabian government but which previously was a major activity of the Bedouin. *Al-ghazzu,* the raid, is distinguished by the Bedouin from *al-harb,* war, since the raid was intended to capture camels from tribes of equal status. Āl Murrah did not raid each other nor lower status tribes, but all other noble tribes of Arabia were open to attack. War could occur between tribes or against nontribal groups in efforts to obtain territory or to subjugate another group or to pillage, but *al-ghazzu* was supposed to be carried out only between noble tribes and was supposed to be reciprocal. The Āl Murrah claim that they took almost all of their best milk camels and riding camels from other tribes in raids but that they were seldom raided themselves. Because they raided the northern tribes and then escaped back to the Rub' al-Khali, they were indeed less open to counterraids. As a result, they probably reciprocated less than other tribes which lived in the more densely populated north. Because fighting was kept at a minimum and people were killed only rarely and because it was reciprocal among equal status tribes, one author (Sweet 1965) has seen this phenomenon as a mechanism of exchange in the desert that served to keep herds relatively equally distributed. Since the development of the centralized state, however, *al-ghazzu* exists only in the poetry and folklore of the tribe.

TRIBAL LEADERSHIP

As we have seen, the basic subdivisions of the tribal structure are the lineages, referred to by the Bedouin as *fakhds,* thighs. In contrast, there are the *'aynin,* the eyes, who are the tribal leaders. But in practice among the Āl Murrah, the tribal leaders are only slightly differentiated from the rest of the tribe. The Āl Murrah are strongly egalitarian. Their leaders function as first among equals and are members of lineages and clans just like all members of the Āl Murrah. They are respected and consulted for advice on both traditional and modern matters. They rule by persuasion and not by threat of physical force, and their continuation as leaders results from their ability to reconcile conflicts within the tribe and to successfully represent the tribe in dealing with the outside world. In the past, they were powerful military leaders who depended on the support of the tribe. Today, they mainly depend on their ability to work as intermediaries between the tribe and the government.

Three different groups of people have provided paramount leaders for the whole tribe. The first were the Āl Muradhaf of the Āl Jaber clan. Then there were the Āl Nagadan of the Āl 'Athba clan and now there are the Āl Shoraim of the Āl Fuhaidah clan. The Āl Shoraim have been the paramount leaders of the Āl Murrah since the beginning of this century. The other two groups continue to be closely involved with their own clans, but they recognize the present pre-eminence of the Āl Shoraim. The Āl Ghurfran clan is led by the Āl Bu Lailah. All of the members of these groups, each one of which is a subdivision of a lineage, or a minimal lineage, have the social status of shaikhs, a status which in Saudi Arabia is occupied by major religious leaders, ministers of the government who are not of the royal family, and tribal leaders. Among the tribes, the actual leaders are usually referred to and addressed as amirs, a title they share with members of the royal family, governors, mayors, and police chiefs. There are two other minimal lineages which provide amirs for their oases, the Āl Nudailah of the Āl Buheh clan of al-Khinn oasis and the Āl Henzab of the Āl 'Athba clan of as-Sikak oasis. Thus only the Āl Jarabah and the Āl Gayathin clans are without special leaders.

Talib ibn Rashid ibn Shoraim is the present paramount amir of the Āl Murrah. He lives in a black tent indistinguishable from the tents of the rest of the tribe, except that it seldom accompanies the other people during the course of their migrations to fall, winter, and spring pastures, and it only rarely joins the rest of his lineage at their summer wells. Throughout the year, the amir's tent stays in the rolling sands ten to twenty miles west of the town of Abquaiq and within a few hundred yards of the Riyadh-Dhahran highway or the spur that connects al-Hasa to that highway. This area is one of Arabia's richest oil fields and the nights are unceasingly lit by the gigantic flares of burning natural gas.

The amir's household keeps a few camels in milk and a small flock of sheep and goats for milk and for feasting, which he does on a large scale (he entertains almost nightly). The rest of the amir's camels are entrusted to other tribesmen who herd them and live off them as their own. The area in which the amir pitches his tent provides relatively good grazing, but he does not select this area out of any concern for pastoralism. He selects his campsite because of its convenient location close to the towns of Abquaiq, Dammam, and Hofuf, the capital of al-Hasa oasis. His business as tribal leader calls him to one of these towns almost daily. His campsite can be easily found by Āl Murrah coming from other places.

Except for short periods in the winter and spring, when they migrate to pastures in the north, the amir's household is joined by those of his close relatives who share in his status and in his duties. These include the household of his eldest son, Rashid, and his mother, the amir's first wife; that of one of his father's brother's sons and his mother; and that of another father's brother's son. The previous amir of the Āl Murrah was the father's brother of the present amir. Thus the amir is joined by his sons and the sons of the previous amir. All of these men work closely together, and the amir is almost always accompanied by one or more of these young men in everything he does. The amir himself is illiterate but his sons and his father's brother's sons all have been to school (one completed secondary education and the others, intermediate level).

The duties of the amir include being the commander of a reserve unit of the Saudi Arabian National Guard, for which he receives a salary and the use of vehicles. Although people from other tribes are members of this unit, the mass of them come from the Āl Murrah, with a large proportion of these coming from the amir's clan, the Āl Fuhaidah. This unit is mainly residual and only meets regularly for a few days each month during which time the members receive their salaries, approximately 450 riyals ($100) per month. They are always on call, however, and can be easily brought together in about two days, even from deep inside the Rub' al-Khali. Aside from being an important source of cash, the National Guard unit serves as the major focus of tribal life and is a major information center. Since all the clans are represented, news about political affairs and about pastoral concerns—especially news about the rains—is easily passed on to all sections of the tribe.

The amir also serves as a kind of *wasta,* intermediary, between the individual tribesman and the government. If a person is arrested for any reason, the amir immediately becomes involved in the case, almost as a *de facto* lawyer for the defendant. He spends at least half his time discussing cases with the amirs of al-Hasa and the eastern province of Saudi Arabia, and in some instances, he must go to the capital in Riyadh to discuss a case with high governmental officials or the king. Most of the infractions are minor—many of them resulting from automobile accidents—but they also include assault and murder. Also, the amir speaks not only for the members of his own tribe but for several smaller tribes from the Najran area who traditionally accepted protection from the Āl Murrah. Within the tribe, the amir plays the role of arbitrator, and when conflicts between groups occur, he works hard to reconcile both parties and to reach a peaceful settlement. If he cannot reconcile them, he will go with them to a powerful member of the royal family to seek his opinion.

None of the amirs are presently active in any of the pastoral activities of the tribe, although they own herds of camels and sheep and goats. In the past, they played a more active role, and the ancestors of the present amir are said to have organized and protected Āl Fuhaidah migrations into the grazing areas of northeastern Arabia during the last century when intertribal conflicts were common. Amirs were also active in organizing work projects in the four oases the Āl Murrah possess. The only subsistence-related activity of tribal importance which the amirs practice today is the use of their influence with governmental officials to obtain new wells or to repair and modernize the old ones. Their advice is actively sought by the tribesmen, especially about contemporary changes.

The position of amir is an achieved status which can be maintained only through the continued success of the leader and his close relatives. That this is so is evidenced in the rise to power of the Āl Shoraim. According to the Āl Murrah's version of their own history, the Āl Muradhaf were the paramount chiefs of the tribe when the tribe had its urban focus on Najran in southwestern Arabia. About two hundred years ago, the Āl Murrah, under the general leadership of the Āl Muradhaf, expanded northeastward out of the Rub' al-Khali and took the oasis of Jabrin by right of conquest from the Dawasir tribe. The Āl Muradhaf and their clan, the Āl Jaber, consolidated themselves in this oasis while other elements of the tribe continued pushing northward. The Āl Fuhaidah clan was particularly active in this push because, according to the Āl Jaber, they were poor in camels or, according to the Āl Fuhaidah, they were brave warriors. Indeed, the finest milk camels of the Āl Fuhaidah, those of the Āl 'Azab lineage, were taken in raids against the Mutayr tribe in northeast Arabia during the last 150 years. The Āl Shoraim's rise to pre-eminence dates from the nineteenth century and is considered by the Āl Murrah themselves to be directly related to the expansion of the tribe as far north as al-Hasa, which has displaced Najran as the urban focus of the tribe as a whole. They became the paramount chiefs of the Āl Murrah because they did not establish themselves at Jabrin but because they made themselves felt in the rich and important oasis of al-Hasa.

Both *al-harb wa as-siyasiya*, warfare and diplomacy, were major factors in the rise of the Āl Shoraim. They were active in tribal warfare in the desert regions around al-Hasa. Nearly every mountain and hill in the vicinity of the oasis is named for a battle fought between the Āl Murrah and other tribes such as the Beni Hajir, Manasir, and Dawasir for access to grazing areas in the desert regions around al-Hasa. The Āl Shoraim capped their pre-eminence in tribal warfare with diplomacy, not with other tribes, but with the administrators in al-Hasa. They are often described as entrepreneurs who entered into discussions with the Turkish rulers of al-Hasa in the nineteenth century. One of the Āl Shoraim was to be named governor of the oasis by the Turks, but on the eve of his nomination, he was murdered by members of the Beni Hajir while walking in the streets of the oasis. Subsequently, the Āl Shoraim allied themselves with the Āl Sa'ud and played an important role in the conquest of al-Hasa from the Turks in 1911. Their relationship with the oasis was also cemented by a marriage between a woman of the Āl Shoraim and Fahd ibn 'Abdallah ibn Jiluwi Āl Sa'ud, the eldest son of the governor of al-Hasa and the eastern province of Saudi Arabia, who was King 'Abd al-Aziz ibn Sa'ud's cousin. The Āl Muradhaf lost their pre-eminence during the latter part of the nineteenth century and first decades of this century by remaining in Jabrin and by continuing to focus their extra-tribal attention towards Najran rather than towards al-Hasa, which was destined to become a key center in the present-day Kingdom of Saudi Arabia.

As the rise of the Āl Shoraim indicates, the activities of successful leaders are very much related to affairs beyond the realm of internal tribal ones, and include an involvement with the greater political and social world of the state. Today, their principal activity is as mediators between the state and the tribe. Their role in leading wars against other tribes has disappeared within the last fifty years since the Āl Sa'ud imposed peace throughout the area. Yet, all the amirs of the Āl Murrah remain intimately tied in with the affairs of the Āl Murrah. They spend almost all of their time in the company of fellow tribesmen, even when traveling to cities. Their material standard of living is slightly higher; they have pickup trucks and cars and are not dependent on the vagaries of pastoralism. They have important ties with powerful urban-based officials, but their dealings with these officials are exclusively concerned with tribal matters.

Rather than working for personal aggrandizement—which they could easily do—the amirs work with political and legal problems concerning the tribe. They have not been particularly outstanding in promoting the economic and social development of the tribe, perhaps because the older amirs, including the paramount amir, are products of traditional Arabia and have had no more experience with modernization than have the camel nomads. Furthermore, development programs initiated under the auspices of the government and other agencies have never actively attempted to incorporate these leaders or their sons into the planning or execution of development programs.

The Āl Murrah amirs are not necessarily opposed to change. They are aware of the changes that have been taking place since the development of the oil industry, especially since World War II, and they are very much concerned for the future of the tribe. Unfortunately, the younger members of these families do not receive the kind of training or education that would be of help to them in comprehending the vast social and economic changes that are such a prominent feature of contemporary Saudi Arabia, and that would allow them to work towards the incorporation of their tribe into a modernized society. Instead, they are experiencing a deep personal frustration with changes which appear to be leaving them by the wayside. This is a problem the sons of amirs face but which that their age-mates in the tribe do not experience. Their fathers are very much interested in the intricacies of traditional tribal politics and have made their whole lives within this context. Their children, however, have gone to school, have spent long periods in the rapidly changing cities, have traveled abroad, and are interested in the modern world of which their tribe is hardly a member. They feel a strong bond with the tribe, but they also feel that they are different because of their schooling and urban associations. They want to become involved in modernizing the tribe, but they don't know how to begin or how to fit into the development process. At best, some are full-time National Guardsmen, performing duties which are not far from traditional. At worst, they have nothing to do. As in most developing countries, one of the most difficult problems is the mobilization and utilization of the unique human resources of the country in the development process. Some of the most able and highly motivated individuals are bypassed for responsible positions in favor of bureaucrats whose only credential is that they have spent more time within the walls of a school than the bright young people who are supposed to be the beneficiaries of development.

The classic descriptions of segmentary societies are the works by Sir Edward Evans-Pritchard on the Nuer (1940), a group of cattle herding pastoralists in southern Sudan, and on the Sanusi (1949), in which he discusses the Bedouin of eastern Libya. More recently, scholars have begun to indicate the inadequacy of viewing these and similar societies exclusively, or mainly, in terms of segmentation, in which all groups are balanced and unite and separate according to the process of fission and fusion based only on patrilineal descent. Salim (1962), for example, has shown that among the Marsh Arabs in southern Iraq, the clan of the chief is much larger in number and vastly more powerful than the other clans, although in ideology they are equally descended from the tribal founders. Fernea (1970) has stressed the separateness of the shaikhs from the rest of the tribesmen in southern Iraq and has also shown how the social, practical, and religious community of the tribes includes nontribal market people and governmental administrators as integral members of their community. Peters (1968) has called attention to the stratification of tribes in Libya into the free and the tied, or into patron and clients, and has indicated the theoretical importance of this phenomenon. The highly stratified tribes of Iran can hardly be understood in terms of the segmentary system, although this system is operative among the average tribespeople.

Internally, the dynamics of Āl Murrah social organization closely approximates that of the classic models of segmentary societies. All of the lineages are roughly the same size and are roughly equal in power and wealth. The amirs are not highly differentiated from the rest of the tribe, although as they achieve more wealth and education, as a result of the development of a modern economy in Saudi Arabia, they may begin to be more differentiated. That wealth and power are equally distributed throughout the Āl Murrah tribal organization is a consequence of the pattern of ecological adaptation they have established. The size of a household's herd does not vary widely, since the carrying capacity of the land and of wells is limited, and, after a certain minimum is achieved, there is little to be gained from having a large herd. The Āl Murrah keep camels for subsistence and only rarely exchange them for cash or barter in any markets. Thus there is neither capacity nor incentive for amassing or hoarding wealth and, as mentioned earlier, the pattern of migrations they follow does not require special military protection or the special services of any centralized authority. Because they are camel nomads and because the environment they inhabit demands it, they must be highly flexible and each unit must be independent and able to fend for itself, alone in a vast desert for extended periods of time. In sedentary situations, tribal leaders can easily take advantage of their position and concentrate wealth and power in their hands as in the two Iraqi examples. In Iran, powerful chiefs with independent armies have important roles to play in guaranteeing the movement of the tribe from one area to another across hostile territory. But in the case of the Āl

Murrah, the amirs play almost no role in the daily activities of the camel nomads. Their importance lies in smoothing their relationships with the outside world, which as we will see, their economy demands.

The segmentary lineage system is both a kinship system and a form of political organization. Indeed, we might say that it is essentially a form of political organization that relies on the principles of kinship for bringing people together in political action. People join together in group endeavors because they are related through kinship—not because of any study of issues, as in an ideal democratic society, nor because of force, as in authoritarian societies. Defense groups are mustered according to degrees of kinship and all the descendants of a common ancestor fight together. Major work parties are similarly organized on the basis of common descent. Even who you drink coffee with or who you visit first depends on kinship—a person, for example, visiting a camp different from his own always goes first to the tent of his nearest patrilineal relative rather than to that of one who may be a closer friend or even the person he has immediate business with. This system is characterized by a high degree of independence and egalitarianism at every level. Leadership is based on persuasion rather than any kind of physical force that tribal leaders command, and tribal leaders operate as first among equals rather than as a highly differentiated group of people.

It would be a mistake, however, to equate the total political system of the Āl Murrah, or any other Bedouin, with the segmentary lineage system. Among themselves, it is the major way in which coalitions, for whatever purpose, are brought about, but ties based on alliances through marriage and with one's mother's relatives often have a great deal of influence in political action (although these kinds of ties are not given formal recognition). Externally, and even in a few instances within the tribe, differentials in status are major determinants of action. The Āl Murrah, with the exception of a couple of tainted lineages, are of *sharif*, noble, status in Arabian society and join together as equals with other *sharif* tribes in many situations in which genealogical relationship is not taken into consideration. Ignoble or subservient tribes are treated with condescension, even when they are sometimes addressed as kinsmen. The total political structure of the tribe must also take into consideration the wider society and especially the existence of the state, a subject we turn to in the following chapters.

The social structure of the Āl Murrah is characterized by the inclusion of more and more people as in a series of concentric circles. In the center is the household, then the lineage, the clan, the tribe, the nation, the Arab world, and the world of Islam. Each circle brings more people into relationship with the household in the center. That the household is an autonomous and independent unit at the center of their social world is a consequence of their ecological adaptation as camel nomads. Each household owns and is exclusively responsible for its own herd, the basis of their subsistence. The other units of their society provide them protection and a general framework within which to organize their herding activities on a regular basis. But their situation demands flexibility, and the household quite often has to operate entirely on its own. The segmentary system, which provides for household autonomy instead of lineage or tribal dominance, provides this flexibility.

Chapter 5

THE ĀL MURRAH AND
THE WIDER SOCIETY

Bedouin tribes are often conceptualized as discrete, well-bounded social units which enjoy a high degree of autonomy in all spheres of life—cultural, social, economic, and political. The Bedouin, however, must sometimes come to the city because their life is not now—and probably never has been—self-sufficient in the desert. There are certain basic, universal needs which can only be satisfied in the city. While the Āl Murrah are highly self-sufficient in their most important staple food, milk, they depend on the city for an essential part of their economic well-being. There are also services of primary ritual significance which are tended to most frequently and easily in the city. Politics, too, often calls them to the city.

Aside from camel herding and subsistence sheep and goat herding, there is little that the Āl Murrah perform for themselves without the involvement of urban-based functionaries or specialists. In the northern parts of Saudi Arabia, where there is a much higher concentration of nomadic pastoralists than in the areas normally inhabited by the Āl Murrah, there are groups of non-pastoralist nomads who perform specialized services for the pastoralists. These include the Sulluba, who because of their blond features and their custom of tatooing a cross on their wrists, are believed by some to be descendants of some lost Crusaders. The Sulluba hunt and sell what they procure to the Bedouin and townspeople of northern Arabia. They also work as blacksmiths and repair all manner of items. Their women are reputed among the Bedouin to work as prostitutes. They are considered to be of decidedly lower social status, since the selling of food and the dependence on working for others are considered highly degrading. Others who perform services for the Bedouin in the deserts of northern Arabia include itinerant merchants, religious specialists, and schoolteachers. None of these functions are available to the Āl Murrah in their sparsely populated territories. They depend on the city of Hofuf for most of these services.

The traditional relationship between the Bedouin and the wider society can be characterized as one of mutual interdependence. Just as the Bedouin depend on the city for many essential services, the traditional city (and the village) depended on the Bedouin for protection. In recent decades, these services have been taken from the Bedouin, usually by force, and transferred to the centralized state. But prior to the establishment of a strong state, individual Bedouin tribes guaranteed the protection and security of specific cities and villages, as well as lower status nomadic groups and craftspeople. Although those who were protected sometimes speak of the Bedouin as exploiters, since their protection was often only against other Bedouin, the positive features of this system should not be overlooked. As Abdalla Bujra has clearly shown for South Arabia (Bujra 1971), the urbanite, the villager, and the Bedouin together participated in a complex web of social, economic, political, military, and religious relationships—many of which continue into the present, though often in drastically changed and changing form.

ECONOMIC RELATIONSHIPS

The Āl Murrah maintain close economic ties with two major Saudi Arabian urban centers—Najran, which is their traditional hometown, and Hofuf, which has become their most important urban focus since the latter part of the nineteenth century. Almost all of their material necessities are now obtained by cash or credit purchase in the *suq*, marketplace or bazaar, of Hofuf, which is the administrative center of al-Hasa oasis.

The major food items they purchase are dates, rice, flour, onions, tomato paste, and salt. Coffee, tea, cardamom, sugar, perfume, and incense are essential items in their social activities and are regularly purchased in Hofuf. Cloth, ready-made clothes, and footwear are also purchased here. All of the items they use in herding—leather buckets and troughs, ropes, saddles, wooden blocks and pulleys for their wells, bamboo camel sticks—are obtained here. Many of their household items—coffee pots, tea-pots, cooking utensils, trays, and cups—are at one time or another purchased. The women buy rings and gold and silver jewelry from jewelers in the *suq*, and the men obtain bejeweled daggers and guns and ammunition.

Although they regularly purchase a wide variety of items, the Āl Murrah seldom sell any of their own products. The women do collect camel's wool and make it into yarn which they sell to merchants in Hofuf. Occasionally an individual brings a camel to sell in the camel market in Hofuf. But these sales account for only a small and irregular part of their income. The money for most of their purchases comes from military pensions, salaries for participation in the Reserve National Guard, and, increasingly, from wage-labor. Most of the Āl Murrah also receive a part of the date harvest of al-Hasa oasis which is channeled to them through the office of the amir of al-Hasa. The tribal amirs also receive special payments of money and dates from the amir of al-Hasa and from the king at the end of the fast of Ramadhan.

Since they obtain most of their income through government payments rather than the sale of their pastoral products, it is tempting to say that they are supported by welfare and leave it at that. But the situation is more complex. Before the discovery of oil and the development of a modern cash economy, economic exchanges in Arabia were effected without the widespread and general use of money. Different segments of the populace received specialized goods and services in exchange for those of other segments. The traditional specialists of the Bedouin are military protection and pastoralism, services they customarily have extended to the sedentary commercial, craft, and agricultural sectors in return for payments in goods and services from them. The military protection the Bedouin afforded these sectors prior to the establishment of a strong centralized state cannot be under-estimated. Their military might guaranteed the security of villages, caravans, and major market towns. The Āl Murrah, for example, traditionally guaranteed the *suq al-khamis*, the Thursday market, the major market day in Najran and their closely related tribe, the Āl Hindi, guaranteed the smaller *suq al-ithnayn*, the Monday market, in Najran. In return, they received part of the harvest of the oasis of Najran and special payments from merchants and craftsmen. None of the villagers or urbanites were traditionally armed nor did they know how to fight. Thus in the absence of state police, they relied on the military specialists of Arabia, the Bedouin.

Since the creation of the modern state of Saudi Arabia during the first decades of this century, the tribes have been incorporated into the military structure of the state, a process we discuss in greater detail in chapter 6. Thus they continue to be paid for their military support. What has changed is that instead of a direct relationship between a tribe and a village or a tribe and a market-town, all of the tribes have been incorporated into the National Guard which is commanded by and serves the interests of the centralized state of Saudi Arabia and thus the total nation. Payments are channeled to the Bedouin mainly through the National Guard by the central government in return for their military services.

The Bedouin have also maintained economic relationships with sedentary folk that do not involve military protection. Many sedentary folk own animals which they entrust to the Bedouin to fatten in winter pastures. The herders have the right to any milk the animals produce while they are herding them. Many Bedouin own agricultural plots in oases that are cultivated by sedentary farmers who share the harvest with the Bedouin owners. In most cases where this kind of economic exchange occurs, the sedentary folk claim to be descended from the same ancestors as the Bedouin and are thus members of the same tribe.

POLITICAL RELATIONSHIPS

The political relationships that tie the Bedouin into the wider society have already been alluded to in discussing their specialized military role. Although the tribes formerly maintained a high degree of political autonomy, as Muslim tribes they have always recognized the theoretical sovereignty of religio-political authorities that stand above the tribal structure. Since the creation of the modern state of Saudi Arabia under the aegis of 'Abd al-Aziz ibn Sa'ud, the father of the present-day King Faisal, the Bedouin recognize the legitimacy of the Saudi Arabian state. They proudly and readily say they are Āl Murrah, Āl Faisal, People of Murrah of the People of Faisal, which obviously utilizes their segmentary model to relate themselves to people with whom they do not share kinship but with whom they unite as the followers of King Faisal.

The Āl Murrah distinguish between two aspects of the modern Saudi Arabian state—the *dowla,* by which they mean the modern bureaucracy, and the *hukuma,* by which they mean the members of the Āl Sa'ud royal family and a few other leading religio-political families. They consider themselves to be the special supporters of the *hukuma* as the rightful leaders of an Islamic nation. The *dowla,* the bureaucracy, which they recognize to be rapidly increasing in power, is a factor worth some concern.

Leading members of the *hukuma* (sg. *hakim,* judge or ruler) have traditionally played crucial roles in the mediation of conflicts both between tribes and among elements of the same tribe. Since the first decade of this century, the Āl Murrah have had close relationships with the Āl Jiluwi branch of the Āl Sa'ud who have provided the rulers of al-Hasa and the Eastern Province. Conflicts among the Āl Murrah and between them and others are almost immediately brought to the *hakim's* attention, and in most cases it is he who mediates or renders a judgment which theoretically must later be ratified by a *qadi,* a religious judge. As shown in chapter 4, the tribal amir of the Āl Murrah plays the part of a spokesman or lawyer on behalf of his tribal followers in their dealings with the *hukuma.* Cases which cannot be decided by the provincial rulers are taken to the king.

The Āl Murrah's relationships with the *hukuma* include marriages. Women from families of amir status marry members of the *hukuma* and thus symbolize and help to cement political alliances between the tribe and the *hukuma.* The offspring of these marriages take the status of their father's family but their relationships with their mother's tribal relatives are carefully maintained and cultivated, even for generations after a particular marriage. The Āl Shoraim have marriage relationships with the Āl Jiluwi branch of the Āl Sa'ud and with the Āl Thani rulers of

Qatar. The Āl Muradhaf have marriage relationships with the Āl 'Abdurahman branch of the Āl Sa'ud and the Āl Nagadan with the Āl Thani.

RELIGIOUS SERVICES

The third major way the Bedouin are tied into the wider society of Arabia is through religion, which is the subject of the following chapter. Suffice it to note here that many services religious in nature can only be satisfied or accomplished in the city. These include marriage contracts, circumcision, curing, and the payment of the *zakat*, a religious tax. The Āl Murrah have no religious specialists among themselves and for all of these services they have to come to the city—almost always Hofuf.

Marriage requires recourse to religious authorities in the urban area since the union must be approved by a shaikh of Islam before one can formally consider the union binding. Prior to the celebration of the actual wedding, the groom or his representative and a representative of the bride approach a shaikh of Islam and tell him of the planned marriage. He inquires into the relationship between the bride and groom—to avoid incest—and asks about the willingness of the bride to be married. If he is satisfied that everything is in order, he grants his approval. The groom can then take possession of the bride, usually at a feast celebrated at a later convenient date in the desert.

Religiously prescribed male circumcision is performed on prepubescent boys by an *'umtowa*, a minor religious figure. The mother of the boy takes her son to the *'umtowa* to whom she pays a small fee. After saying a few ritual prayers, the *'umtowa* cuts the boy's foreskin. Among the sedentary folk, circumcision is an important rite of passage which is celebrated with a great deal of fanfare. Among the Āl Murrah, it occasions no special activities—perhaps because it takes place in the city far away from the tents and one's people.

Many of the Āl Murrah rely on several *'umtowas* in Hofuf who are individually renowned for their curing abilities. The Āl Murrah practice a rudimentary system of medical treatment based on cauterization, and they deal with such things as superficial wounds and childbirth in the desert. They rely entirely, however, on urban based *'umtowas* and modern doctors for any complicated cures, often consulting both for any serious illness. Teeth are usually pulled in Hofuf by professional dentists, even though this may require a trip of over 400 miles from the Rub' al-Khali. The rare cases of acute insanity (only one occurred while I was with them) are dealt with by religious functionaries in Hofuf. Special readings of the Koran are read to the victim.

Representatives of Āl Murrah households visit the town of Hofuf about once a month. Most of them come towards the end of the lunar month, which is when they receive their salaries from the Reserve National Guard. The *suq* in Hofuf becomes a major gathering place for people from all the clans and lineages of the Āl Murrah. The Amir Talib, who often has to go to Hofuf on business with the amir of al-Hasa, makes his headquarters in the shop of a merchant whose ancestors his ancestors protected in the days before centralized government. In a way the *suq* in Hofuf is the social center of the Āl Murrah. Hundreds of tribesmen converge there to make their purchases and to pay their debts. They meet members of lineages that they never encounter in the desert. They greet their tribal brothers and exchange news.

The Āl Murrah, like all the other Bedouin in Saudi Arabia, depend on the city and the wider society for many things that are basic to their lives. But the Marri does not love the city. For whatever reasons bring him there, he makes his stay as brief as possible. He concludes his business and returns to his herd in the desert as soon as he can find a pickup truck going his way. It is an understatement that he does not feel at home in the city. He spends restless nights there bothered by mosquitoes; he rarely has any milk to drink; he easily catches cold during the winter; and, more importantly, he feels no kinship or sense of community with the average native of the city. He sticks with whatever tribal relatives he can find and together they talk of camels and the desert. He goes to the city because he must, never because he likes it. And when he leaves, he and his companions inevitably burst into song as soon as they get past the outskirts of the city and off the paved roads.

Chapter 6

RELIGION AND THE WORLD OF ISLAM

In the late fall of 1968, only a few months after I had joined al-Kurbi's family and household in the Rub' al-Khali, Merzuq, his younger brother, and I were driving a herd of about seventy full-grown camels across a wide plain with only a few dried clumps of grass. News had come of good rains in the north, and we were beginning the migration back to Bir Fadhil before going on towards the north. Merzuq glanced at the sky and called out to me that it was time to pray. While the rest of the camels drifted on eastward, we turned our mounts to the west, tapped them on the back of the neck with our bamboo camel sticks, uttered gurgling sounds to make them kneel down, and dismounted.

With his stick, Merzuq drew the outline of a mosque in the sand, with the half moon circle facing towards the west, towards the Ka'aba in Mecca: ◡. Each of us individually knelt down, placed the palms of our hands in the sand, and made motions as if we were washing our faces. He rose and asked me if I wanted to call the prayer. I deferred, and he clasped his hands to his mouth and called in a loud voice to any that might hear in this vast solitude: *Allahu akbar, allahu akbar, ashadu wallah illah il allah . . .*

Allah is Great! Allah is Great!
I witness that there is no god but Allah.
I witness that there is no god but Allah.
I witness that Muhammad is the messenger of Allah.
I witness that Muhammad is the messenger of Allah.
Come to Prayer! Come to Prayer!
Come to Prosperity! Come to Prosperity!
There is no god but Allah.

Then we stood side by side, with me to his right because I was less knowledgeable in Islam, and we silently repeated the *Fatiha,* the opening chapter of the Koran:

In the name of Allah, the Beneficient, the Merciful.

Praise be to Allah, Lord of the Worlds,
The Beneficient, the Merciful.
Owner of the Day of Judgment,
Thee (alone) we worship; Thee (alone) we ask for help.
Show us the straight path,
The path of those whom Thou hast favoured;
Not (the path) of those who earn Thine anger
    nor of those who go astray.

We repeated a few other short verses. Several times we knelt down and touched our foreheads in the sand. After the last prostration, we sat for a few moments before we turned to our mounts and Merzuq challenged me to a race to see who could catch up with the herd first.

Most descriptions of the Bedouin and of other nomadic pastoral peoples in the Middle East state that religion is not a major concern of these people. They point out that they seldom pray and that they know and care little about the religion of Islam, to which all of the Middle Eastern nomads formally adhere. One study of an Iranian tribe speaks of "a ritual life of unusual poverty" (Barth 1961:146). While the Āl Murrah are by no means well versed in the theology of Islam and are little given to mystical contemplation, Islam is an integral part of their lives. Their's is a simple, straightforward version of the religion, but it is one that fits closely with the rhythm of life in the desert. Their close adherence to its rituals is important to them, and they cherish that its truth have been revealed to them.

ISLAM

Islam had its beginnings in the urban environment of Mecca, an important trade center in western Arabia, during the first two decades of the seventh century A.D. Although its roots are tied to the culture and society of the Arabian Peninsula and its language is Arabic, Islam is strongly universal in its appeal. It draws its believers from societies as diverse as Indonesia, the Philippines, sub-Saharan Africa, Iran, Afghanistan, Pakistan, Turkey, and the Arab world. It is one of the world's fastest growing religions today and claims a following of at least one billion people.

In its beliefs, Islam draws heavily on many elements of Judaism and Christianity, but its stress on the essential oneness and abstract, incomprehensible nature of Allah, literally the God, is unique. Islam itself means submission or resignation, and Muslims are those who have submitted or resigned themselves to the will of Allah. In Islam, there are no specially chosen people, no saints, and no God in trinity—Father, Son, and Holy Ghost. It is highly egalitarian in ideology and in its internal organization. All believers are considered to be equal; there is no special priesthood. The essence of Islam is said to be found in *at-Tauhid,* the Unity, one of the last chapters of the Koran:

> In the name of Allah, the Beneficient, the Merciful.
>
> Say: He is Allah, the One!
> Allah, the eternally Besought of all!
> He begetteth not nor was begotten.
> And there is none comparable unto Him.

Its basic requirements, known as the Five Pillars of Islam, include witnessing that there is no god but Allah and that Muhammad is the messenger of Allah; praying five times daily; fasting during the lunar month of Ramadhan; paying a tithe; and making the pilgrimage to Mecca at least once, if at all possible. Although Islam has known a great flowering along with the development of sophisticated religious sciences since its original inception in seventh century Mecca, the formal religious precepts of the Āl Murrah and other Arabian Bedouin remain close to the simple straightforward religion of Muhammad and his followers, as expressed in the Koran, the Holy Book of Islam.

At least one Muslim scholar has pointed out that "Muhammad's message was inspired . . . not in a Bedouin atmosphere but in the commercial *milieu* of Mecca, and that the Qur'an was, indeed, severely critical of the Bedouin character" (Rahman 1966:2). This analysis is true. From a political and sociological point of view, the beginnings of Islam can be explained as an attempt to develop a new community based on universal criteria rather than on the more parochial concerns of the tribe. The Mecca that Muhammad knew was ruled by an elite group of merchants from the Quraysh tribe who, in their greed to enrich themselves, had forsaken the tribal ideals of sharing their wealth with their tribal followers and protecting the poor and indigent. Many of Muhammad's early activities were directed against the power of this ruling elite of his own tribe and in favor of the poor and dispossessed of Mecca. Many of his later activities, especially after the Flight from Mecca to Medina in 622 A.D., were devoted towards setting up a state organization in which all Muslims would be equal without regard to their origins. As the anthropologist Eric Wolf has said,

The religious revolution associated with the name of Mohammed permitted the establishment of an incipient state structure. It replaced allegiance to the kinship unit with allegiance to a state structure, an allegiance phrased in religious terms. It limited the disruptive exercise of the kin-based mechanism of the blood feud. It put an end to the extension of ritual kin ties to serve as links between tribes. It based itself instead on the armed force of the faithful as the core of a social order which included both believers and unbelievers. It evolved a rudimentary judicial authority, patterned after the role of the pre-Islamic soothsayer, but possessed of new significance. The limitation of the blood feud permitted war to emerge as a special prerogative of the state power. The state taxed both Muslims and non-Muslims, in ways patterned after pre-Islamic models, but to new ends. Finally, it located the center of the state in urban settlements, surrounding the town with a set of religious symbols that served functionally to increase its prestige and role. [Wolf 1951:352–353]

But while Muhammad's may have been an attempt to surplant a tribal social structure with a more universal one, and while the Koran may be often critical of the Bedouin character, the influence of the Bedouin is strong in early Islam, and Islam today still fits well with the traditional rhythm of life in the desert.

Many of the injustices that Muhammad fought against were those of a tribal elite which had lost contact with the average desert dweller. As so often happens even today, the ruling elite had separated itself from its tribal kindred and no longer followed the egalitarian ideals of the tribe. By seeking to increase personal wealth and power, the elite felt hampered by the demands of poorer relatives. Muhammad is said to have spent several years of his youth with the Bedouin and it is surely from these experiences that he gained much of his feeling for social justice. His humanism, in my opinion, is not that of a refined urban sophisticate but is more like that of the Bedouin who judge a person, whatever his station in life, by his honesty and his straightforwardness. To the Bedouin of today, any man who acts in a devious, deceitful manner is despised, however high his status. They treat people as equals but judge them according to how they act.

The relationship of the Bedouin to the political world of Islam has had a topsy-turvy history. After the firm establishment of the religion in Medina, Muhammad's followers began to preach among the Bedouin and the other people of Arabia. Soon after the death of Muhammad in 632, they began the conquest of the rest of southwest Asia and north Africa. Armies composed mainly of Bedouin tribesmen from Arabia quickly conquered most of the Byzantine Empire and Iran and established a far-flung Islamic Empire that eventually reached from Spain across north Africa and southwest Asia to India and China. The center of religious learning and political power shifted from the Arabian Peninsula first to Damascus and then to Baghdad and eventually to Cordoba and Cairo. Until the last three decades, Arabia remained a backwater within the political and religious world of Islam. Those Bedouin and others who did not migrate with the early armies of Islam remained for a millenium in an isolated and impoverished desert region, and are said to have lapsed back into an almost pre-Islamic way of life.

RELIGIOUS REVIVAL AND THE
CREATION OF THE STATE OF SAUDI ARABIA

As early as the eighteenth century, however, things began to stir in Arabia as a religious revival movement began, once again in an urban environment. One Muhammad ibn 'Abd al-Wahhab traveled from a town in central Arabia to Mecca and Medina and then to Basra in southern Iraq. He diligently studied the Koran and other writings, and he soon became convinced that the Bedouin and the townspeople of his home regions were Muslims in name only. They followed too many superstitions, and instead of worshiping Allah alone, they also prayed to stones and trees and believed in the special powers of saints, both living and dead. He returned to his homeland, and in 1741 he began to denounce these practices publicly and to preach for a return to the teachings of the Koran. He soon gathered a group of followers, and in 1744 entered into a special alliance with Muhammad ibn Sa'ud, the ruler of Dara'iya, a small oasis town near present-day Riyadh in central Arabia.

The pact that Muhammad ibn 'Abd al-Wahhab and Muhammad ibn Sa'ud entered into was at least partially based on the teachings of a medieval reformist, ibn Taimiiya, who had envisioned an ideal Muslim society that would contain two classes of authority: "that of the 'ulama', who possess knowledge of the Law, and that of the 'umara', holders of the political power necessary for its application" (Laoust 1939:294; my translation). Together the Āl Sa'ud and the Āl 'Abd al-Wahhab (now known as the Āl ash-Shaikh) pledged themselves to fight for the reform of religious belief and practice and the establishment of an Islamic state. This alliance still holds today, with the descendants of Muhammad ibn 'Abd al-Wahhab occupying most of the major religious posts and the descendants of Muhammad ibn Sa'ud controlling the major political ones.

The establishment of such a state, however, did not come easy. Historians describe Arabia at this time as being in a general state of anarchy. The Ottoman sultans claimed control of the Holy Cities of Mecca and Medina in the Hejaz, but local administration of this area was in the hands of the Hashemites, descendants of the prophet Muhammad. The Yemeni highlands, the area of Najran, and Oman were ruled by different dynasties, each one of which followed rival Islamic sects. In eastern Arabia, the chief of the Beni Khalid Bedouin tribe dominated the oases and caravan routes of that part of Arabia. Much of the rest of Arabia was rent by a division between the Bedouin and the townspeople. Many of the Bedouin tribes and many towns, as well, sought to remain independent and as a result were often at war with each other.

The reform initiated by Muhammad ibn 'Abd al-Wahhab was essentially puritanical. Such vices as tobacco, alcohol, luxurious clothing, singing and dancing, and raucous behavior of any kind were strongly condemned. Laxity in the performance of religious rituals was not tolerated. As a result, the Wahhabis, as his followers were called, gained a reputation as dour, puritanical religious fanatics. Nonetheless, the call to a return to orthodox Islam attracted growing numbers of followers, especially in central Arabian towns. It also attracted a great number of dissidents, many of whom were Bedouin tribesmen. Military expeditions began to be formed by the reformers to further not only the reform of Islam but the establishment of a centralized state. During the next two centuries, until 1932 when the modern state of Saudi Arabia was officially created, the Āl Sa'ud in alliance with the Āl ash-Shaikh fought to control and to bring political and religious reform to Arabia.

At some times, as between 1792 and 1814, they dominated much of Arabia and spread out to threaten southern Iraq and Syria. In 1918, however, they were conquered by Egyptian forces who razed their capital at Dara'iya and took their leader, 'Abdallah ibn Sa'ud, to Istanbul, where he was executed as a rebel against the Ottoman Empire and for Wahhabi attacks on the religious elite of Mecca and Medina. During the rest of the nineteenth century, the Āl Sa'ud struggled to regain their control of Arabia, and between 1840 and 1891 they were relatively successful. Between 1891 and 1902, however, the Āl Sa'ud lost control to the Āl Rashid, who were the leaders of the Shammar Bedouin tribe. During this period, the then young 'Abd al-Aziz ibn Sa'ud and other members of his family lived in exile, at first with the Āl Shoraim, the family of the amir of the Āl Murrah, and later in Kuwait. Finally in 1902, 'Abd al-Aziz left Kuwait and, in a bold attempt, recaptured the city of Riyadh and began another long fight to reestablish a centralized state, culminating with the creation of the Kingdom of Saudi Arabia in 1932.

The participation of the Bedouin in the long struggle of the Āl Sa'ud and the Āl ash-Shaikh to establish a centralized Islamic state in Arabia was extremely varied and often contradictory. In this regard, it is useful to refer to the ideas of Ibn Khaldun, the famous fourteenth century Tunisian scholar who is often hailed as the world's first sociologist. He developed a model to explain the way in which the Bedouin, during the early centuries of Islam, interacted with the central religio-political authorities. According to Ibn Khaldun, the Bedouin are proud and unwilling to acknowledge another's superiority. They are difficult to lead except when they follow a prophet or holy man, for religion alone can diminish their haughtiness and restrain their jealousy and competition.

According to his scheme, the Bedouin interact with the sedentary people according to a cycle of four stages. During the first stage, the Bedouin unite in religious zeal with certain elements of the sedentary population and establish themselves through conquest as the rulers of a certain area. Usually the sedentary folk take the main political and religious offices and the Bedouin occupy military posts. The second stage is characterized by the consolidation of the state throughout the area and the continuation of a high degree of puritanical religious zeal. During the third period, the arts and sciences experience a high degree of development and religion becomes less puritanical. The Bedouin also begin to lose interest in the whole enterprise and begin to drift back to their nomadic pastoral activities. The fourth period is a long one of general decline, during which the Bedouin forsake the state and return to their semi-anarchic existence in the desert.

The late Sir Edward Evans-Pritchard, in his classic study of the Sanusi Islamic reform movement in Libya during the nineteenth and twentieth centuries, sheds a great deal of light on the participation of the Bedouin in religious reform movements. The original success of the Sanusi Brotherhood in Libya was due primarily to the fact that they developed an organization of lodges that paralleled the segmentary structure of the tribes in Libya. Each lodge, composed of members of the Sanusi Brotherhood, was attached to a particular section or lineage of a tribe. Thus they created the foundation for a supratribal national organization that did not attempt to alter the basic tribal structure at the same time that it incorporated the tribes into a more universal structure, that of the Sanusi Brotherhood.

In Arabia, the Āl Sa'ud and the Āl ash-Shaikh sought drastic changes among the Bedouin and their incorporation into the structure of the new Islamic state. As a result, some of the Bedouin were sometimes for them and sometimes against them. The reformers won their major victories against rival powers primarily because of the fearless fighting of religiously inspired Bedouin armies. At the same time, one of their most powerful internal threats was the very same Bedouin and their tribal amirs. Ibn Khaldun's observations of a thousand years ago about the unwillingness of the Bedouin of early Islam to acknowledge another's authority and the difficulty of leading them were just as true in the first two decades of this century when 'Abd al-Aziz was attempting once again to bring unity and centralized authority to Arabia.

THE *IKHWAN*

In previous chapters, I have discussed the rhythm of life of the Āl Murrah as determined by the seasons and the needs of their herds. I have implied that this occurs with a high degree of regularity and that external political and economic factors have little effect on the actual pattern of herding. This was the situation I experienced during the two years I lived with them and, from statements of the Āl Murrah, this situation has prevailed for at least a generation. However, before the final consolidation of the modern state of Saudi Arabia in the 1930s and 1940s, the political climate within which the Āl Murrah and the other Bedouin of Arabia operated was much less peaceful and serene. Raids and counter-raids, feuds, and small-scale wars between tribes and against villagers were more the order of the day. The genius of 'Abd al-Aziz ibn Sa'ud lay in his ability to bring order throughout the disparate regions of Arabia and to incorporate the often warring and rebellious tribes into the structure of the state which he created.

The ideology that 'Abd al-Aziz drew upon was that of Islam as taught by the Wahhabi reformers. Unlike the Sanusi reformers in Libya, who attached themselves to the segments of the Libyan Bedouin tribes without attempting to change the tribal structure, the Āl Sa'ud and the Āl ash-Shaikh attempted to effect major changes in the religious beliefs of the Bedouin and in the basic structure of their society and economy. This involved a major program of teaching and preaching for the conversion of the Bedouin from their so-called infidel practices to what they believed to be the true version of Islam. Many believed that nomadism itself was incompatible with the life of a true Muslim, since it seldom provided the opportunity for performing ritual ablutions regularly and since it was usually impossible for the Bedouin to attend schools to learn to read the Koran.

The major organization created by 'Abd al-Aziz for bringing about these changes among the Bedouin was the *Ikhwan al-Muslimin,* the Muslim Brotherhood. Starting around 1912, he convinced the Bedouin to establish perhaps as many as 200 *hujar,* settlements, throughout desert Arabia. These new towns were a combination of military camp, agricultural colony, and missionary center. Their inhabitants, known to each other as *Ikhwan,* Brothers, probably included a majority of the Bedouin of central Arabia. Although the development of agriculture was supposed to be one of the major goals of these communities, this was the most neglected sphere of their activities. Their major achievements lay in the spread of fundamentalist Islam among the Bedouin and the creation of a standing army of *mujahidiin,* Holy Warriors, ready to fight under the banner of the Āl Sa'ud and in the name of Islam at a moment's notice.

The participation of the Āl Murrah in the *Ikhwan* was generally half-hearted. Their territory is an isolated one and far-removed from the major centers of action in central Arabia. While many of them were intensely interested in the politico-religious movement of the *Ikhwan* and all of them were affected by their preaching, most of the Āl Murrah found it impossible to completely abandon their camels for sedentary life in agricultural colonies. Four *hujar* were established by members of the Āl Murrah at Jabrin, al-Khinn, as-Sikak, and an-Nibak, but none of the Āl Shoraim, the paramount amirs of the tribe, nor any of their fellow clansmen participated in the *Ikhwan* or ever attempted to settle. Many of the Āl Murrah did participate in the military activities of *Ikhwan* armies, but only a few of them became actively involved in the movement on a full-time basis. Also, ecological factors plagued the four Āl Murrah *hujar* from the very beginning, since they were ridden with malaria and did not have sufficient water resources for large-scale agriculture.

The major tribes which were most active and influential in the *Ikhwan* were the Mutayr, the 'Atayba, the Harb, and the Shammar, all of which are located in the northern half of Arabia. Each of these tribes is associated with the development of large and successful *hujar* under the leadership of members of their chiefly families. Although sedentarization was voluntary, 'Abd al-Aziz was apparently more interested in settling and pacifying some tribes than others. The Mutayr, for example, had been particularly active in raiding in northeastern Arabia, and they were one of the first to be induced to settle. In late 1912 and early 1913, many of the Mutayr were convinced by Wahhabi preachers to sell their camels and horses in the market in Kuwait and to take their new wealth and build a new community for themselves in the wadi of al-Artawiya. They were taught that nomadism was against true Islam and that they should abandon their wandering and their internecine raiding and feuding to settle down to culti-vate and to study their new-found religion.

That the Mutayr and others were so easily convinced to aban-don the means of their pastoral existence and to settle in new com-munities is at least partly explained by the special obligation they had to participate in *jihad,* Holy War, against unbelievers. Not all of the tribe completely abandoned pastoralism and some of the members of each of the new *hujar* concentrated on pastoral activities. Most of the able-bodied men, however, were on per-manent call for immediate participation in any *jihad,* and *Ikhwan* armies under the command of their own amirs were responsible for the major military victories that led to the establishment of the new state of Saudi Arabia. In so doing, they combined the skills of endurance and of fighting they had learned in the desert with the zeal of religion. They fought bravely and wildly, com-pletely without fear, against regular armies that were much better armed than they and that usually outnumbered them many times.

The most spectacular victories of the *Ikhwan* armies were in the Hejaz in 1924. Armed with only a few primitive rifles and their old-fashioned daggers, they fought against the well-supplied regular army of the Hashemite rulers of Mecca and the rest of the Hejaz. They quickly vanquished them in hand to hand battle and took the city of Taif in the mountains above Mecca. The *Ikhwan* army, mounted on camels, then marched with their guns pointing towards the earth to Mecca, which they occupied with-out firing a single shot. 'Abd al-Aziz and the rest of the Āl Sa'ud soon followed and accepted the surrender of the Hashemites and declared 'Abd al-Aziz king of the Hejaz.

Flushed with their victories here, many of the *Ikhwan* were eager to carry on the struggle against those who differed from their version of Islam. Members of the Hashemite family were on the thrones of Trans-Jordan and Iraq and were in close collaboration with the British, who were obviously infidels. As a result, some of the *Ikhwan*, on their own initiative, began to raid against both Trans-Jordan and southern Iraq. The British responded with air raids and threatened 'Abd al-Aziz to either contain the *Ikhwan* within his own country or suffer attack by the British.

The relationship between the *Ikhwan* and the Āl Sa'ud had not always been smooth. As mentioned earlier, 'Abd al-Aziz's reason for creating the *Ikhwan* was a desire to transform the tribes from semiautonomous units, each with its own body of warriors, into a force that would be loyal to him and to the new central state which he was attempting to establish. The ideology for this new state was at first based entirely on Islam, but as 'Abd al-Aziz began to consolidate his control over Arabia, he began to speak more and more in secular terms. At first he had taken the title *Imam*, which is a religious title meaning leader of a religious community. Later on, he took the more secular title of sultan and eventually the purely secular one of *malik*, king. During the same time, he was forced to choose between following strictly the letter of the Koran and the *Sharia'*, Islamic holy law, or adopting new practices that were more in accord with the modern world. In the field of education, he opted for a combination of modern secular learning and religion rather than establishing a purely religious education system, as many of the religious leaders had wanted.

Many of the *Ikhwan*, on the other hand, became more fanatical and vigorously rejected such modern inventions as the automobile, the telephone, and the telegraph as inventions of the devil or his followers. 'Abd al-Aziz insisted on the need to bring modern secular education and modern technology into Arabia. As a result, many of the *Ikhwan* became disillusioned with him and ceased to believe that he was likely to establish the kind of Islamic state they had been led to believe in. They were particularly convinced of this when he sought to contain their advances against Trans-Jordan and Iraq and when, in the fall of 1929, he subdued them in battles in which he relied upon armies composed of members of the traditionally sedentary population who were not members of the *Ikhwan*.

This account of the *Ikhwan* has been necessarily brief. What is important for us to note is that autonomous or even semiautonomous tribalism in Arabia was erased, probably forever. Reformist Islam was a major factor in early efforts to incorporate the tribes into the structure of a centralized state. But when the armies of the *Ikhwan* began to act independently and without the approval of 'Abd al-Aziz, who had transformed himself into a secular leader, they were crushed by armies that owed allegiance only to 'Abd al-Aziz as the ruler of a secular state.

Another factor that is often overlooked in the demise of the *Ikhwan* is the widespread failure of the new communities to develop agriculture successfully. The nomadic pastoralists who settled had no knowledge of agriculture and little enthusiasm for learning about it. Moreover, the water resources were often insufficient to support any large-scale development. They had only primitive means of drilling shallow wells which were incapable of tapping deep water resources. As a result, many of the new communities completely exhausted the water reserves that were near the surface of the ground and were forced to abandon the sites of their new communities. Thus ecological factors forced many of those who had settled to return to the desert and the herding of animals to sustain their own subsistence.

Those who returned to full-time herding faced a very different situation from that which had prevailed in the days before the *Ikhwan*. The independent military power of the tribes was completely broken. Many had been outright defeated by armies of the Āl Sa'ud, and their horses, their major means of transportation in military endeavors, were either confiscated or killed. Those who had not been militarily defeated were nonetheless induced by the Āl Sa'ud to get rid of their horses and to refrain from any military activities that were not under the leadership of the Āl Sa'ud. Raiding of other tribes and the harassment of travelers were strictly forbidden and offenders were severely punished by the police of the new state.

The old system of tribal justice was also completely undermined. In the past, legal decisions among the Bedouin had been made according to customary tribal rules. Their judge, known as an *'arifa*, was any wise man or sage who knew the customs of the tribes; his judgments were not backed up by physical force but were implemented by public opinion. From very early on, however, the Āl Sa'ud declared that the *Sharia*', Islamic holy law, was the only acceptable legal system. All other practices were considered infidel. An extensive system of religious courts was developed and Islamic law was strictly applied. Today, all legal decisions fall within the formal jurisdiction of the *Sharia* courts.

ISLAM AND THE BEDOUIN TODAY

The outcome of the decades of upheaval that preceded the emergence of the modern Kingdom of Saudi Arabia as it exists today is probably not what any of the major participants in the religious reform movement headed by the Āl Sa'ud and the Āl ash-Shaikh envisioned. Certainly the secular power of the state, largely monopolized by the Āl Sa'ud, has overshadowed the power of the *'ulama'*, the religious scholars, although the latter are still an important force in contemporary Saudi Arabian society. Islam continues to be the major ideological force, and instruction in the precepts and beliefs of the religion occupy a major part of the school curriculum. Legal decisions are based formally on the *Sharia*', and the *'ulama'* are formally consulted on many state decisions. But the reality of the modern world has brought many innovations to Arabia and quite often governmental officials can only rely on the Koran and the teachings of Islam for inspiration in a general sense rather than in the sense of finding a precedent for some action.

Some of the more conservative and religiously oriented townspeople are critical of the Āl Sa'ud for encouraging the introduction of modern changes in Arabia and for not sharing power more equally with the *'ulama'*. This is not a criticism made by the Bedouin, however. They praise 'Abd al-Aziz and the Āl Sa'ud for bringing peace and security to the desert and for the benefits that have been passed on to them through the development of the economy. They remember their past as one of poverty and insecurity. Today they no longer live in eternal fear of raids, and the standard of living has been greatly improved, a factor we will discuss in greater detail in the next chapter.

Perhaps the most successful aspect of the *Ikhwan* movement was their missionary activity among the Bedouin. The eminent geographer Alois Musil, who traveled throughout northern Arabia and lived for a time among the powerful Ruwalla tribe during the first few years of this century, stated that at that time few of the Bedouin could even recite the beginning verse of the Koran and that few of them prayed regularly or gave much thought to religion. In 1914 he visited a town, al-Jauf, just conquered by the Ruwalla and was amazed at how much the *Ikhwan* missionaries had taught the Bedouin and how religious they had become (Musil 1927:427). Today the Bedouin remain steadfast in their performance of Islamic rituals and are eager for more knowledge about the religion. They no longer display the fanaticism of their fathers and grandfathers who fought in the *Ikhwan* armies and believed that the automobile, the telephone, the telegraph, and other modern inventions were the creations of the devil. Indeed, many recognize that the fanaticism of the *Ikhwan* was based on ignorance and an improper understanding of Islam.

Earlier I said that the Islam of the Bedouin is a simple, straightforward version of the religion that fits well with the rhythm of life in the desert. The Bedouin are not given to esoteric or mystical thought. Their survival depends on their own skills and then continuous hard work, and as a result, they are highly pragmatic in their approach to the world. They seldom, if ever, attribute specific happenings to witchcraft or sorcery or other extraordinary powers. None of their people are considered to have any special or supernatural powers and they have no special religious personnel. They believe in the existence of the *jinn*, spirits, and *shetan*, devils, because the Koran says they exist and because they have heard numerous folk tales about them. But many of the Āl Murrah I knew were skeptical, since they had never individually come into contact with these beings.

The misfortunes that befall the Bedouin are seldom individual ones. Only during the days of raids was an individual likely to lose all or most of his animals through negligence—and this he could rectify by raiding others. The misfortunes the Bedouin experience are more likely to be general and to result from forces over which they have no control. Prolonged droughts affect all of the Bedouin in any given area equally, as does the spread of disease among their animals. Locusts, before they were brought under control by the international campaigns against them during the last two decades, often brought ruin to the Bedouin as they consumed all the vegetation, leaving nothing for the animals. Conversely, the Bedouin have little control over years of plenty: it either rains and grasses and shrubs are in abundance and their animals become fat, or it doesn't and their animals become lean and even die.

The Bedouin see themselves as part of a world ruled by an ultimate power over which they have no control or influence and which they do not question. Allah is the supreme power, the Ruler of the Worlds. Unlike the God of the Christians who is anthropomorphized and often referred to as Our Father, the Allah of the Muslims is never anthropomorphized but is considered to be an abstract absolute force, the nature of which is incomprehensible to human beings. Allah's presence is manifest in all things and in all acts, seen and unseen, and the Muslim is the one who totally resigns himself or herself to the will of Allah. Every Muslim is equal before Allah, and no intermediaries, such as priests or saints, stand between the individual and Allah.

The abstract quality of Allah and the rejection of priests and saints are perhaps the most compromised aspects of Islam in its popular manifestations. The 'ulama' have usually adhered to the official teachings of Islam, but the intermediation of saints and special holy men have often been important factors among the less educated populace of many Muslim countries, especially among peasants. The popular religion of the Bedouin of Arabia, however, remains close to that of orthodox Islam, which stresses the equality of all Muslims before an all-powerful and essentially incomprehensible God. This orthodoxy is partly a result of Wahhabi preaching, which lays great stress on these aspects of Islam and vehemently opposes giving special reverence to or worshiping or believing in the special supernatural powers of any person or thing other than Allah. It also accords well with the reality of their desert life.

The day begins among the Bedouin just before sunrise with the call to prayer. An old man, usually, who tells the time by the place of the stars in the heavens, gets up and in a loud voice calls the morning prayer. While the women pray individually in their part of the tent, all of the men gather at the mosque, which is nothing more than a place drawn in the earth just to the east of the tent. Whoever is most knowledgeable in Islam, because of age, special study, or the number of times he has made the pilgrimage, leads the prayer. Just as it is finished, dawn begins to break in the east and the camp begins to stir. Morning coffee is roasted and brewed, and people gather to discuss the activities of the rest of the day—whether they will move or, if not, where the camels should be taken to graze.

As the sun climbs in the sky, the day begins to warm rapidly and soon the tent is struck, if they are moving, or the camels are taken off to graze. The warmth steadily increases, the winds usually die down, and things become still as the sun climbs to the zenith. When it is overhead and a person casts no shadow, once again the call to prayer rings out. Those who have remained in the camp gather at the mosque at the edge of the tent and pray silently, making their prostrations towards the Ka'aba in Mecca. The herder, alone with his camels, draws a half moon circle in the earth and silently prays and prostrates himself. The heat of the day is at its maximum now and those in the camp seek refuge inside the tent where they doze. The camels off in the desert lie down and doze and chew their cuds. The herder looks for the slight shade of a bush and sleeps there for an hour through the midday heat.

As the sun passes the zenith, brief afternoon winds often blow up, and then as the sun begins to go down, the heat of the day lessens. The camels are roused and are turned back towards the camp. The people in the tents awaken, and two hours before sunset the call to prayer sounds out again. People pray again, coffee fires are built, and socializing at different people's tents begins in earnest. At sunset, the prayers are called once more. At this time, the prayers are usually longer and are prayed out loud by the leader. Two hours later, the fifth and last prayer of the day is again prayed.

The day of the Bedouin is thus punctuated by prayer. In the cities, modernist elements of the populace sometimes complain that the five prayers interfere unnecessarily with the rhythm of modern urban life. They interrupt business and school, and most people hate to rise before dawn, especially since the modern work day does not begin for several more hours. In the desert, however, there is no conflict between the time of the prayers and the rhythm of herding. Indeed, the prayers seem to fall at natural divisions in the day. The Bedouin traditionally divide the day not into hours but into the periods defined by the prayers. For example, a man says that he saw such and such a person just before the midday prayer, or that it took him from the time of the mid-afternoon prayer until the sunset prayer to get from here to there.

The belief in an abstract all-powerful Allah also corresponds well with the reality of the desert life of the Bedouin. Many non-Muslims think of Islam as exceedingly fatalistic due to its emphasis on the total power of Allah and its belief that all things are *maktub*, written, i.e., preordained by Allah. The forces over which the Bedouin have no control and which affect their very survival—droughts and years of plenty, pestilence and disease—are all cosmic forces and are obviously not under the control of any individual or group of people. They live very close to nature. The yearly rhythm of their life is determined by the seasons and the daily rhythm by the alternation of day and night and, during the day, by the position of the sun, and the consequent degree of heat, and the winds. One praises Allah for the blessings of a good year and resigns oneself to the misfortune of a bad year, without seeking scapegoats among one's fellows. Fortune and misfortune, over which one has no control, are both attributable to Allah. The Bedouin, however, think that it is very much their business to work hard with what they have. They know that one who abandons his camels, even only occasionally, is courting misfortune. They know that others do not possess their herding skills and their knowledge of the desert, but their skills and knowledge they attribute to experience and learning, not to any special gift from Allah. They are thus fatalistic with regard to happenings over which they have no control. Concerning phenomena over which they do exercise some control, they are pragmatic realists.

Observance of the five daily prayers is only one of the Islamic rituals that the Āl Murrah and other Bedouin of Saudi Arabia strictly observe. Fasting during Ramadhan is an important annual event in their religious and ritual life. Ramadhan is the lunar month that is set aside to commemorate God's revelation of the Koran to Muhammad. During this month, Muslims refrain from eating and drinking and from sexual intercourse during daylight hours. The nights, however, are dedicated to feasting and socializing with family and friends. The fast is not intended as an atonement for sins or a punishment of the body, as in the Christian Lent, but it is a joyous occasion for celebrating Allah's gift of the Koran. The days are supposed to be spent in religious contemplation and in reading the Koran while the nights are spent in social celebrations that, through the sharing of food and festivities, reaffirm social relationships.

The Āl Murrah celebrate Ramadhan according to the season in which it falls, as the Muslim lunar calendar is approximately eleven days shorter than the solar year. When Ramadhan falls during the summer, a considerable degree of hardship is experienced, since the days are very long and the summer heat increases one's thirst. But the summer nights, with most of one's lineage mates together at the wells, are joyous occasions with large communal feasts each night. During other seasons, the camps are smaller and the feasts consequently much smaller in scale. In whatever season, however, special efforts are made to obtain special foods, and each night everybody gathers to break the fast just after sunset. A larger meal is served a few hours later and, just before daybreak, everyone partakes of another meal and drinks a big bowl of camel's milk to sustain himself through the coming day. The 'Id al-Kabir, the Big Feast, is celebrated after the end of Ramadhan by putting on new clothes, dancing to Bedouin war songs, running foot races, and in many instances culminating with a camel's race.

The other major ritual that is the goal of everyone is the pilgrimage to Mecca. Before the introduction of modern means of transportation, the observance of the pilgrimage was often an exhausting and time-consuming project. Few of the Bedouin were able to cross the more than a thousand miles of desert between eastern Arabia and Mecca. Nowadays, however, with trucks and greater monetary resources, many of the Bedouin are able to make the pilgrimage more than once and everyone makes it at least once in his or her lifetime.

During the first winter I spent with the Āl Murrah, I accompanied a group of them part-way on the pilgrimage. 'Ali, the old man in whose tent I resided, his wife, al-Kurbi, eighteen other men and women of the Āl 'Azab lineage, and I traveled in a pickup truck from eastern Arabia to Riyadh and then to Taif, where I stayed while they went on to Mecca. The trip itself was a major event. Normally, one can travel from eastern Arabia to Hejaz in one day or a day and a half by automobile. Our journey took ten days. We continuously stopped for long breakfasts, lunches, and dinners which were totally prepared on the spot.

Often we met other groups of the Āl Murrah who were also making the pilgrimage and had to stop to socialize with them. The highway was filled with buses, trucks, and cars from Kuwait, Iraq, Iran, Afghanistan, and Pakistan. Some were filled with exotic looking tribal people, more or less the equivalent of my companions. Others were sophisticated urbanites in sleek modern automobiles. In Taif the motorized caravans from the east were joined by Yemenis from the south coming in trucks and some by camel caravan, as in days of old. From the north, buses filled with Turks, Syrians, Jordanians, Palestinians and Lebanese converged on Mecca. Airplanes and ships brought pilgrims from Africa, Indonesia, the Philipines, and even America. Official figures indicated that over a million people made the pilgrimage that year.

I could not travel with them to Mecca because officially I was not a Muslim, although the Āl Murrah considered me to be one with them in spirit. When they returned, they had bought watches, mint and other spices, fabrics for clothing, and perfumes and incense, showing that the commercial side of the pilgrimage still remains since pre-Islamic times, when tribes put aside all their conflicts to exchange goods at an annual fair held within the precincts of the city. But the major events in Mecca were the circumambulation of the Ka'aba, the huge black stone that legend says was the abode of Abraham, the casting of stones at mythical devils in the town of al-Minna just outside Mecca, and the sacrifice of an animal on the plain of Arafat to commemorate God's substitution of an animal when Abraham was going to sacrifice his son Ishmael.

Within the precincts of Mecca, all divisions of social status and national origin are obliterated. Everyone wears the same type of clothing—a seamless white shroud wrapped around the waist and draped over one shoulder. Women do not wear veils and participate equally in the performance of all rituals. People from vast regions of the world, of different colors and languages, rich and poor, modern sophisticates and traditional tribal peoples, leaders of nations and exploited peasants and workers, unite as equals before God and reaffirm their belief that there is no god but Allah and Muhammad is his messenger.

When my friends returned from Mecca and met me in Taif, they were all in a state of excitement and happiness. The two old men who traveled with us had both made the pilgrimage in 1924 as members of the *Ikhwan* army which conquered the Hejaz. They were happy and felt themselves privileged to have come back in more peaceful times and in greater comfort to perform this important ritual. The younger members of our group were also very much impressed by the masses of people and the excitement of the ritual. True to their Bedouin spirit, none of them had had their shoulder-length hair cut, a traditional feature of the pilgrimage for many sedentary people. They all felt that they had fulfilled an important duty in their life. Unfortunately, our return trip was marred by an accident in which our truck turned over twice. Miraculously, none of us were hurt seriously and no one was killed (although anyone who dies while on the way to or from the pilgrimage is assured entrance into paradise). After a month, we finally returned to Āl Murrah territories and to tearful receptions by those who had stayed behind. The performance of the pilgrimage does not confer any special social status back home among the Bedouin, as it does in some other societies where the *Haji,* the pilgrim, is specially revered. Among the Bedouin it is simply a requirement for all people. Its performance gives individual satisfaction and a heightened awareness of the power and unity of Islam, but not social status.

Islam enters into the lives of the Āl Murrah in a number of other ways. The only tax they pay is the *zakat,* an alms tax, the payment of which is one of the five Pillars of Islam. This is a kind of graded income tax—the amount one pays is determined by the wealth one possesses. Thus a man with less than five camels pays nothing on them, but a man would pay one ewe on five to nine camels, two ewes on ten to fourteen camels, three ewes on fifteen to nineteen camels and so forth. In recent years, cash equivalencies have been established for this tax. Payment of the *zakat* is a social obligation and is the evidence of one's submission to rulers who carry out the Law of Allah Most High. The Āl Murrah pay their *zakat* annually to the ruler of the eastern province of Saudi Arabia.

Islam also plays a part in many life crises. Male circumcision is performed on young boys when they are five or six years old, in accordance with religious belief. Usually the Āl Murrah take their young sons individually to a man in Hofuf who performs the operation. Unlike many sedentary people in Arabia who have a big celebration at this time, the Āl Murrah do not have special festivities to celebrate the circumcision. Marriage involves the approval of religious authorities and must be registered in the religious courts to be legally binding. Attitudes towards death are very much influenced by Islam. Death is not mourned, since it is seen as the will of God and since the believer goes to paradise, for God

> . . . hath awarded them for all they endured, a
>   Garden and silk attire;
> Reclining therein upon couches, they will find
>   there neither (heat of) a sun nor bitter cold.
> The shade thereof is close upon them and the clustered
>   fruits thereof bow down.
> Goblets of silver are brought round for them, and
>   beakers (as) of glass
> (Bright as) glass but (made) of silver, which they
>   (themselves) have measured to the measure (of
>   their deeds).
> There are they watered with a cup whereof the mixture
>   is of Zanjabil,
> The water of a spring therein, named Salsabil.
> There serve them youths of everlasting youth, whom,
>   when thou seest, thou wouldst take for scattered
>   pearls.
> When thou seest, thou wilt see there bliss and high estate.
> Their raiment will be fine green silk and gold
>   embroidery. Bracelets of silver will they wear.
>   Their Lord will slake their thirst with a pure
>   drink.
> (And it will be said unto them): Lo! this is a reward
>   for you. Your endeavor (upon earth) hath found
>   acceptance.   [Koran LXXVI:12–22]

How different their heaven is from the life they lead in the desert! Consider, for example, the difference between the heavenly pleasures described in the Koran and the mundane exigencies of their life during Ramadhan. I remember the first Ramadhan I spent with the Āl 'Azab, deep inside the Rub' al-Khali when we were beginning the migration to the north. Al-Kurbi had taken some of the heavier household items and his mother and father and the children to Bir Fadhil in the truck. Muhammad, Merzuq, bint Batahan, a man from the Āl Jaber clan, and I went with the camels. Towards the end of the first day, about two and a half hours before sunset, when it was still and hot, I was so tired and thirsty that I felt like collapsing. We had pitched camp and I went over to where the big rubber innertubes with water were. I looked at them and longed for a drink. There was no one around. But I didn't have a cup and I knew it would be obvious if I untied them and drank. I lay down in the sand by a bush and bided my time. Every muscle ached from having ridden camelback all day long. I wondered why I was there and why I had decided to live like them. Anthropology and Berkeley, where I was a student, couldn't have seemed farther away.

About an hour before sunset, Muhammad came up and said "Let's make coffee and prepare for breaking the fast after sunset." My attention from my bodily desires was diverted while we built a fire, roasted coffee beans, and then pounded them to powder and brewed coffee. Soon it was sunset. We gave bint Batahan part of a pot of coffee which she drank by herself. The man from the Āl Jaber, Muhammad, Merzuq, and I took cups and broke the fast. The coffee was bitter because we had made it with water from a brackish well, but that was minor to the relief it gave once it was drunk. It was already cool now, and after we prayed, we sat and talked while bint Batahan prepared a meal of rice with a rabbit that Muhammad had shot during the day.

After a while she brought us the tray of rice with the rabbit on top. We gathered around and murmured "In the name of Allah, the Beneficient, the Merciful" and began eating with our right hands. It was delicious. Afterwards, the man from the Āl Jaber thanked his hosts by praying that their mother and father and all their grandfathers would be together in heaven. We cleaned our hands by rubbing them in the sand and pouring a few drops of water on them. Merzuq brought out some cologne and splashed a few drops on our hands and faces. Then we went back to the coffee fire and Merzuq made mint tea. I wondered if it would be bitter, but it wasn't. He had taken water from another innertube which was better.

After a while, bint Batahan joined us and we lay in the sand around the coals of the fire talking until past midnight, when we drank long draughts of camel's milk. We spent most of the night talking about camels, and they told stories of raids and wars they had heard from their fathers and grandfathers. I no longer felt any fatigue. I was glad I hadn't cheated by drinking water before the end of the day. I couldn't imagine being anywhere else.

On other occasions, I have broken the fast among wealthy sedentary folk and marveled at the vast amount of food and drink. But I have never spent a happier Ramadhan or experienced the joy of breaking the fast at the end of the day so much as when I was with these four young people deep inside the vastness of the sands of the Rub' al-Khali. There was a minimum of ritual and we had only the barest of necessities. But we were very close, and the religion we followed was not separate from the rest of our lives but an integral part of everything we did.

Among the Bedouin deep inside the desert there is no need for big celebrations that bring all the members of a big social group together. Independence of action rather than social solidarity is the first demand of the ecological setting in which they live. Neither Ramadhan, nor birth, nor circumcision, nor reaching adulthood, nor death occasion any special celebrations among the Āl Murrah. Only marriage is associated with an attempt—usually feeble—to bring people together for a special feast. When they are united in big gatherings, they feast together, but as long as one is in the desert, he doesn't need other people. He knows that his lineage, his clan, and the whole tribe is there around him, but he doesn't have to be with them all the time.

Chapter 7

THE ĀL MURRAH AND
THE MODERN WORLD

When I first went to the Rub' al-Khali, I met Hurran ibn Muhammad, a young man about twenty who was not yet married.
As I mentioned earlier, it was Hurran who first put me on a camel
and who challenged me to my first foot race among the Āl Murrah.
He had said that he and I would herd camels together and that
we would go together to look for the daughters of the wind, but,
after that first meeting, I didn't see him again for over six months.
I had gone on with al-Kurbi, and he and his family had gone to
winter pastures far in the north. Since they were from the Āl
'Azab, we knew the general area in which they were pasturing
their camels but we didn't have any direct contact with them
during that winter.

On our return from the pilgrimage and after the accident, we
spent several days in Abquaiq as the guest of the Amir Talib,
who sacrificed a young camel and several sheep to celebrate our
return and our survival of the accident. Then we headed south—
it was spring and the Āl 'Azab were drifting south towards their
wells in the Rub' al-Khali. We were relieved to leave the highways
and the hustle and bustle of the pilgrimage to return to the desert.
We traveled cross-country for several hours and saw a few tents
in the distance and a few herds of camels. Around noon, we

spotted a tent which al-Kurbi and the rest recognized as one of the Āl 'Azab, that of Muhammad, Hurran's father. We stopped our truck about a hundred yards from the tent and began to get out. Suddenly, like a flash, Hurran came running out of the tent. Tears were streaming down his face as he ran to greet everyone. He kissed the old man 'Ali and then al-Kurbi and all of us one by one, including the women, because they were all from the same lineage. We were all crying, too, and he was almost in convulsions. The Bedouin do not cry or become sad when people leave, but when someone comes back after a long absence, they cry from sheer emotion.

Amid the sobs, Hurran said, "By Allah, you will eat meat!" and he started to run into the desert.

'Ali called out to him, "By Allah, Hurran, we will not," and he told one of the young men with us to run after him.

Hurran came back but still insisted that we must stay and eat. He said, tears still in his eyes, "It's been half a year and we've been in the desert and we haven't seen anyone. By Allah, you must eat. The young camel is just here."

'Ali insisted, "Listen, my son, we are all one; your house and my house are one and our herds are one. By Allah, my son, if you sacrifice a camel for us, I swear that I will divorce the old woman."

"But, father, we want you to eat. Please don't swear that."

For Hurran to insist, however, after the old man had sworn that he would divorce his wife, would have been shameful. So, he led us into the tent where he spread out carpets for us to sit on and began to make coffee and tea.

Hurran is an old-fashioned Bedouin youth. He has long straight black hair that reaches past his shoulders and which he washes in camel urine. He parts it in the middle and wraps a white headband around his head to hold his hair in place. He is a bit vain about how he looks and he is proud of his long hair which marks him as a really traditional Bedouin, in contrast to the townspeople who deplore long hair on males. He usually wears a dagger or carries a rifle when he goes out of the tent. He occupies himself almost exclusively with his family's herd and is helped by his sister and one of his younger brothers. He has seldom been to town, except for brief visits to the market in Hofuf.

Most of the rest of the Āl 'Azab youths are very much like Hurran—they are actively hospitable and they love the desert and their camels. Merzuq, the younger brother of al-Kurbi in whose tent I usually resided, is the same age as Hurran and both are equally tied to the desert. They compete to see whose camels are the fattest because they are both proud of their skills at herding. Both excel at other traditional skills—Hurran, for example, is a poet and Merzuq an excellent hunter. But both Hurran and Merzuq have brothers who are strikingly different from them.

Hurran's next younger brother, Salem, does not wear his hair long and seldom spends any time herding. For the last several years, since he was about fifteen, he has been going back and forth to Kuwait where he spends his time with an ever-increasing number of Āl Murrah who are going there in search of work— many of whom are also settling there permanently. He works at odd jobs there and in other urban areas in eastern Arabia. He always says that he prefers the city to the desert, and he is eager to get some skills and to find a good job. He is still illiterate like his brothers in the desert, but he hopes to go to night school and to begin to learn. Merzuq's modernized brother is, of course, al-Kurbi, who for at least fifteen years now has been working from time to time for wages in occupations that have nothing to do with pastoralism or any of the other traditional activities of his tribe. He is now one of the most highly respected young men of the tribe precisely because he is innovative and has been successful in outside activities.

The division between those who follow the camels and stay in the desert and those who tend towards urban life is becoming more widespread among the Bedouin in Saudi Arabia. Divisions occur within the household itself, as in the case of Hurran's family, and between whole groups of Bedouin, as some are changing more rapidly than others. In 1932, when 'Abd al-Aziz ibn Sa'ud created the Kingdom of Saudi Arabia, youths such as Hurran and Merzuq and most of the rest of the Āl Murrah camel herders were not terribly different from the rest of the population. Today, they are an anomaly.

The Arabia of those not-so-long-ago days is essentially gone forever. Then, there were no paved roads, no telegraphs, no telephones, no electricity, no booming cities filled with peoples from outside Arabia, no gigantic gas flares to light the night skies of eastern Arabia. The vast majority of people lived lives that had changed little for millenia: nomads herding camels in the desert;

camel caravans; camel markets; peasants living in isolated, compact mud-brick villages; a few mud-brick towns with forts, mosques, and a few great houses of the sedentary elite; a subsistence-oriented economy which, nonetheless, produced a surplus of camels, sheep, goats, and dates for export. Military raids and internecine warfare between tribes and the insecurity of the peasant populations in the face of nomadic encroachments were also features of this earlier Arabia.

Glimpses of that Arabia can still be seen in some of the villages and even in corners of the cities and among isolated groups of nomads such as the Āl Murrah. But the world has changed for even the most isolated nomad or villager, and they all know that the old Arabia has gone forever. Thus our study of the Āl Murrah cannot dwell just on the traditional aspects of their life, but must include a description of them in changing Arabia. Other writers such as Thesiger (1959) and more recently Polk (1973) lament the passing of traditional Arabia and prefer to travel across the desert by camel. The Āl Murrah love their camels, talk about them incessantly, and live off them throughout their lives, but they prefer to travel long distances quickly by truck and they all praise the Āl Sa'ud and oil for making their life in the desert a bit more comfortable and secure than it was in the other Arabia a few decades ago. Neither Hurran nor Merzuq nor their modernized brothers bemoan the passing of the old days. They all look forward to change and hope for a better life.

OIL AND THE TRANSFORMATION OF SAUDI ARABIAN SOCIETY

The transformation of Arabia from a highly decentralized society in which tribal and regional differences were predominant into a centralized nation-state began well before the discovery of oil in eastern Arabia and, as shown in chapter six, represented an indigenous religio-political movement that utilized traditional models in which religion played the major role in stirring people to action. But soon after 'Abd al-Aziz had created the Kingdom of Saudi Arabia and had consolidated his control over the Bedouin tribes and throughout most of desert Arabia, oil was discovered by American oil companies. They began drilling in 1935, but the first commercially productive field was not discovered until 1938 at Dammam in eastern Arabia. World War II brought production to a virtual standstill, but exploration and production began again after the end of the war and gigantic reserves of petroleum were discovered. Today, the world's largest known reserves of oil are located in eastern Saudi Arabia. Obviously, the income derived from this resource has resulted in many changes in Saudi Arabian economy and society and perhaps has even allowed the Āl Sa'ud to continue to develop and to maintain their centralized control over the country. Otherwise, without major economic changes, we might have expected the tribal groups to reassert their autonomy and to abandon the sedentary religio-political elite they had supported—in accord with Ibn Khaldun's cyclical model.

When oil began to be produced commercially in Saudi Arabia, the country was extremely poor in monetary resources. The economics of both the pastoralists and the farmers operated without the general use of money, and the *zakat* tax they paid the government was usually paid in kind rather than in money. The only sources for government funds were monetary taxes on the export of camels, sheep, goats, and dates and for the right to make the pilgrimage to Mecca. These amounted to relatively insignificant sums and whether 'Abd al-Aziz could have maintained a viable centralized government without recourse to some kind of foreign aid is questionable. Revenues from the export of oil, however, began to provide the government with ever-increasing sums of money. At first, these were modest and most of the profits from the sale of oil went to the Arabian American Oil Company (ARAMCO) which is owned by four American oil companies—Standard of California, Texaco, Standard of New Jersey, and Mobil. Total Saudi Arabian revenues have increased from approximately 2 million dollars annually between 1939 and 1944 to $5 million in 1950, $334 million in 1960, $1.25 billion in 1970 and over $3 billion in 1973. Oil thus dominates the economy, and in 1969–70 income from oil accounted for 48.8 percent of the total gross domestic product, while agriculture (including livestock raising) accounted for only 6 percent and manufacturing 8.5 percent.

The effect of this rather sudden influx of money into Saudi Arabia has been varied. Extreme imbalances in the distribution of this income have occurred, with much of it going to the royal family and their close associates. As a whole, Saudi Arabia still has a low per capita income (only $450 in 1968) and one of the highest infant mortality rates in Asia (22.7/1000 in 1968). In 1966 average daily caloric intake was estimated at 2,080 calories per capita in contrast with Egypt, a rich agricultural land, with 2,770, and the United States with 3,210 (United Nations 1973). But major efforts are increasingly being made in the fields of education, transportation, public health, and urbanization.

The character of the overall Saudi Arabian population is rapidly changing, with the cities growing much faster than rural areas and with large numbers of foreigners migrating into Saudi Arabia. Most modernization efforts have focused on the cities, but the desert has also changed, especially through the development of modern wells that tap apparently large underground water resources and through the introduction of the truck in the desert. These changes are likely to increase tremendously in the next few years. Due to large-scale increases in production and in the price of oil, the Saudi Arabian government now has large reserves of money—approximately $4 billion in 1973—and is now actively concerned with the full-scale development of the country. How do the Bedouin, and the Āl Murrah in particular, fit into this perspective of change?

Although the standard of living of the Bedouin has improved, their position with respect to the rest of the population has slipped and continues to slip. This is not due to any active campaign against them but reflects the way semiplanned development has taken place in Saudi Arabia. Urban centers have experienced the greatest increases in standard of living and many villages are now also experiencing marked improvements, but the Bedouin remain outside the main stream of development.

Perhaps the most significant area in which the sedentary population has far outstripped the Bedouin is in the field of education. In 1968–70, only three young men from the Āl Murrah were enrolled in secondary schools in Saudi Arabia and one in Kuwait. Only a few score were studying in primary schools. Other tribes have a much better record in this regard, but Bedouin youth are still a small minority in secondary schools and almost none have attended universities in either Saudi Arabia or abroad. The only advanced specialized training they are likely to receive is military, through the auspices of the Saudi Arabian National Guard.

This does not mean that Saudi Arabia has not promoted public education. Quite the contrary is true. Primary schools have been established throughout the country, in villages as well as in towns. Some efforts are also made to send primary school teachers to travel with the tribes in the north, where large groupings are common. Increasingly, Bedouin children are going to study in villages, but this means separation from their families. Unfortunately, the school environment is often hostile, since the town children make fun of the Bedouin and think of them as poor and dirty. Many Āl Murrah boys from groups that stay in the vicinity of Hofuf and Abquaiq attend primary school off and on for a few years and then drop out after learning rudimentary skills of reading, writing, and arithmetic.

Education, however, is highly valued among the Bedouin, but it is difficult for them to get an education and remain nomads. This, of course, is a major argument used by governmental officials for encouraging the sedentarization of nomads. I would suggest, however, that special efforts to reach the Bedouin children could be made. Summer programs specially designed for them could be carried out in the oases where many of them camp during the summer. The school at Jabrin, for example, remains open during the fall, winter, and spring with only a handful of students. It closes in June for summer holidays just when the mass of the Āl Jaber clan arrives at the oasis for three months during which neither children nor adults have very much to do.

Special facilities such as dormitories could also be developed for older children wishing to study at more advanced schools in the towns. In 1970, six Āl Murrah boys between the ages of about twelve and sixteen lived alone in Haradh in tin and scrap lumber shacks, doing all their own cooking and housework, in order to attend the intermediate level school there. Many more students could have been recruited if facilities existed for taking care of them. Aside from general education, special training programs for the Bedouin in such areas as animal husbandry and range management could be developed in conjunction with literacy campaigns. Very little encouragement would be needed to attract large numbers of Bedouin youth who are bright and eager to learn but who find it difficult to cope with regular schools that have been designed by and mainly for the sedentary population.

Because of their lack of modern education, the Bedouin are hampered in their ability to take important jobs in the nonpastoral sphere. The best jobs they can aspire to are as taxi drivers or as chauffeurs for important people in the government or for business concerns. In the oil industry, they can only hope to have jobs as skilled laborers after long years of working as unskilled laborers. Almost never can they aspire to an administrative position in either business, the oil industry, or the government, although these are the choice jobs to which most sedentary Saudi Arabian men aspire. The only channel of upward mobility open to the nomads is through the military, but even here they make up the mass of the troops and only a few of the officers. This means that the Bedouin, by default, do not actively participate in any government, academic, or private programs concerned with the modernization of Saudi Arabian society, although they represent at least twenty percent of the total population.

Interestingly, numerous high placed governmental and academic officials, themselves of sedentary background, are aware of and concerned about this widening gap between the Bedouin and the sedentaries, while few of the Bedouin are even aware of it— much less actively concerned about it. Because of their isolation in the desert and their infrequent trips to cities, they have little overall view of the changes that are taking place. Moreover, they have felt improvements in their own specialized sphere of activity, in pastoralism itself, and the modest cash income they receive from wage labor and military service allows them a number of luxuries they never dreamed of before.

The Bedouin continue to accord themselves special status in dealing with high governmental officials and usually circumvent lower echelon administrators in preference for dealing directly with the king or powerful princes. The king and the princes continue to receive them and to accord them favored status in recognition of the past, but bureaucratization of the governmental process is well advanced and continuing in Saudi Arabia, and I doubt that the younger generation of nomads can rely on these special connections with high officials who now must concern themselves more with international and high level policies. While the older Bedouin and King Faisal and the older princes share memories of the old Arabia and of fighting together for the creation of Saudi Arabia, the younger princes, most of whom have studied abroad, and the young Bedouin know little of each other.

The area outside of pastoralism in which the Bedouin have achieved most spectacular success is in transportation. Most taxis in Saudi Arabia are owned and operated by Bedouin or recently sedentarized Bedouin. They also do a great deal of hauling in small trucks. This accords well with their nomadic upbringing, since it allows them freedom of movement and they can work at their own pace without any bosses. Agriculture and purely sedentary jobs have almost no appeal to the Bedouin and are usually considered downgrading. When they seek jobs, they always prefer to work as drivers.

Aside from their activities in transportation and as unskilled laborers, the Bedouin are experiencing change in two major ways, both of which are related to ecological changes resulting from the increasing application of modern technology to the desert environment of Saudi Arabia. Some of the Bedouin are increasingly settling down and abandoning pastoralism, while others are changing their pastoral activities in order to produce animals for sale on the market rather than mainly for their own subsistence. Both processes depend on the development of underground water resources through the drilling of deep wells operated by mechanical pumps, an activity begun in conjunction with the exploration work of the oil companies and now continued by the Saudi Arabian government. The discovery of apparently large underground sources of water of glacial origin has had a major effect on how the desert environment in Saudi Arabia can be used by pastoralists and has also increased the potential for sedentarization. Because the government, most international advisory and development agencies, and the mass of the modern educated public in the Middle East favor the sedentarization of the nomads, let us turn first to that subject and save for last the modernization of pastoralism, which accords more with the traditional skills and adaptation of the nomads.

SEDENTARIZATION

The sedentarization of nomads is an emotionally-tinged issue in most countries which have significant populations of nomadic pastoralists. Mongolia, according to Lattimore (1962), is one of the only countries with a strong nomadic tradition which is actively encouraging the modernization of nomadic pastoralism rather than actively combatting its continuation. Most modern governments feel that nomadism is a thing of the past which has no place in the structure of a modern society. Political and economic criteria are often cited as reasons for encouraging sedentarization, but cultural prejudices also play an important role in the belief that nomadism is incompatible with the modern world. Strangely, the loss of the contributions of the ecological zones which nomadic pastoralists exploit—and which usually cannot be used for agricultural purposes—is seldom even considered.

Because of their mobility and consequent elusiveness, nomads pose problems for states which seek to control them against their will. They are usually difficult subjects for tax collectors and they tend to cross international borders without bothering to obtain the proper documents and without presenting themselves at border check points. In some areas, as between Egypt and Libya, the Sudan and Libya, and across Sinai between Jordan and Egypt prior to the 1967 war, they have engaged in large-scale contraband activities that have been officially decried and blamed on them rather than on those who actively sought to obtain the legally forbidden items which the nomads merely procured and transported. They have sometimes represented major military threats against the central governments of some areas, as in Iran during this century.

Governments argue that it is only with extreme difficulty that they can extend public education and public health measures to the nomadic populations within their territories. But, as we have seen, there is no reason why governments cannot adapt their education programs to the special needs and rhythms of nomadic pastoralists. Health programs can also be extended to nomads and need not always be centralized in towns and cities. Most nomads are willing to travel to the towns or cities for health reasons if they know that facilities exist there—which implies both the need to develop better facilities and to advertise them among the nomadic populations.

Economically, it is argued that the pastoral economies of most nomads are highly subsistence-oriented and that they are only marginally involved in the national economy. They are seen as taking more from the national economy than they contribute. The services that are extended to them and the general nuisance they cause administrators are not readily compensated for by the nomads who more and more seem to live off the largesse of the government than off their own efforts—especially in the oil-rich countries of the Arabian Peninsula and Libya. However, as we will see in the latter part of this chapter, many of the nomads are trying to change their pastoral activities to bring them more in line with modern cash-oriented economies by producing livestock for sale in urban markets where there is an increasing demand for meat. By so doing, they seek to incorporate the ecological zones that have produced for them for thousands of years into the modern national economy, although unfortunately with little governmental encouragement or aid.

Government planned settlement: the King Faisal settlement project

The only major area in which Middle Eastern governments have exerted themselves on behalf of the nomads is in projects designed to settle them in new agricultural communities. Without exception, all of these projects have either been outright failures or have achieved only partial success. The reasons for this, as we should well understand by now, are directly related to the ecology of Middle Eastern countries. To begin with, agriculture is limited, and even where new underground sources of water have been found, the economically successful production of agricultural goods does not immediately follow. In most cases, it takes years of patient and skilled cultivation of the virgin desert soils to bring them to a level of productivity that favorably compares with either the long established oasis and river-basin agriculture of the Middle East or with imported agricultural goods. The Bedouin or any of the other nomadic pastoralists are the least likely components of the total population to possess either the patience or the skills—not to mention the desire—to develop these new agricultural areas. Not only have they traditionally despised agricultural labor, but they also know nothing about it. Their pastoral activities continue to provide them with basic subsistence and they can acquire other amenities through occasional wage labor. There is obviously little incentive for them to abandon pastoralism and to turn to the development of untried and unproven new agricultural endeavors, even when these are generously supported by wealthy governments. Nevertheless, a great deal of energy, skills, and money has been invested in agricultural settlement projects by Middle Eastern governments, and international agencies such as the Food and Agricultural Organization (FAO) of the United Nations continue to encourage such efforts (FAO 1971).

One of the most ambitious, technically best planned, and most sophisticated agricultural settlement projects has been developed within the tribal territory of the Āl Murrah near 'Ain Haradh in the Wadi Sabha. Known as the King Faisal Settlement Project, an area of some 4,000 hectares (approximately 8,000 acres) of former grazing lands has been prepared for agricultural purposes at a cost of approximately 30 million dollars (Uhlig n.d.:15). Initiated by the government of Saudi Arabia as a pilot project in Bedouin settlement, no expense has been spared to turn this track of desert land not far from the Rub' al-Khali into a modern, well-watered agricultural oasis, where, according to original plans, 1,000 Bedouin families were to be settled in eight villages. About 90 percent of these families were to come from the Āl Murrah, with the remaining ten percent to come from the Āl 'Ajman, Dawasir, and Qahtan tribes.

This project was initiated during the early 1960s when many Saudi Arabian nomads had suffered badly from a prolonged drought of at least seven years' duration. Many of the herds of sheep and goats had been decimated, particularly amongst the northern-based tribes. This same period also witnessed an acceleration in the growth of the major cities of the area as the benefits of oil-derived income began to make a heavy impact on the overall economy of the country. Consequently, an increasing number of younger Bedouins began to leave the desert to seek jobs, mainly as unskilled laborers, in the cities and oil fields of Saudi Arabia and the various states of the Arabian Gulf.

The government became concerned for the fate of its nomadic people and sought to improve their living conditions and to establish what it felt would be a more secure basis for their subsistence than pastoralism. Various settlement projects were initiated, but the King Faisal Settlement Project at Haradh was by far the largest and most ambitious. Although the Āl Murrah had been little affected by the drought or by large scale migrations to the cities, the site at Haradh within their territory was decided on because of its known water resources and because it was conveniently located on the railroad, three hours from the potential markets at Riyadh and four from those at the Dhahran-Dammam-al-Khobar urban complex on the coast.

The government acted partially in response to and in accord with advice given it by the Ford Foundation. A report submitted to the Saudi Arabian government summarized what "the Haradh Project's development program objectives" should be, as follows:

a series of changes from:
1. kinship to citizenship
2. isolated camp life to community life
3. nomadic pastoralism to modern farming
4. individualism to cooperative participation
5. traditional technology to modern technology
6. tribal participation as a kinsman to national participation as a citizen. [Smithers 1966:18–19]

The report also states that the Bedouin is a "man who lives for the day, with no concern for tomorrow, and who enjoys peace of mind." The values of "Bedouinism" are described as drawbacks to development. While he "enjoys peace of mind," the Bedouin is seen as a "victim of limitless hospitality" and has "no concern for tomorrow" and "these two social values obviously present problems to development. Two elements—saving and investment— vital for economic development are not part of the bedouin system of values" (Smithers 1966:19).

While the author of this report may have been a victim of his own cultural biases in favor of conscious citizenship (which may be said to be sorely lacking in the Western world) and the primary family as the basic productive unit in a competitive, capitalistic economy, there is no reason to believe that any of the Saudi personnel involved in the program were consciously interested in creating alienated individualists out of the Bedouin. Their aim was altruistic—to create for the Bedouin what they thought would be a better life than nomadic pastoralism. A Ministry of Agriculture survey made of the Bedouins in the Haradh area in 1964 indicated that 90 percent desired to settle and 99 percent of these wanted to live in concrete houses. In 1970, however, when most of the major technological works had been spectacularly finished and much of the area a lush green, no more than two minimal lineages of the Āl Murrah could be characterized as active participants in the program and very few other nomads were associated with the Settlement Project in any way other than as low-salaried wage laborers.

Why had a well-intentioned, technically sophisticated and costly project such as this failed to develop as a settlement for Āl Murrah and other nomads, at least as of 1970? A crucial factor from the time of its inception was a dearth of communication between the nomads and the project planners and developers. A certain lack of communication has always existed between the sedentary and nomadic populations in the Middle East, but this gap has often widened as many of the sedentaries who comprise most of the bureaucracies have been more and more "westernized" and as these increasingly follow questionable advice given them by pro-Western, culture-bound advisors who have little sympathy for and less knowledge about the traditional organization of society in the area. The report submitted to the government acknowledged that very little was known on the subject of "Bedouinism and debedouinism" but at the same time it advised the Saudi Arabian government to spend a vast sum of its money to change completely not only the economic but also the family structure of a major functioning component of Saudi Arabian society. The models envisioned for this new "debedouinized" society were taken directly (though perhaps unconsciously) from Western (American) society in spite of the fact that this society was experiencing major structural upheavals and when a significant proportion of its younger generation was consciously attempting to regain many of the communal characteristics of a tribal, kin-oriented society. The point is that at no time were any of the Āl Murrah ever seriously approached to find out their feelings on the subject of sedentarization and how they would like to restructure their economy and society if they were given the opportunity. They certainly have opinions on these subjects, but no one bothered to develop a serious dialogue with them, mainly because of cultural barriers between the modernized administrators and the traditional tribespeople.

What of the Āl Murrah who did become involved in this project? During 1968–70, immediately prior to the termination of the construction phase of the project, about twenty Āl Murrah males worked as *kuliya*, coolies (their term), on a 200-acre demonstration and training farm. About ten members of other tribes also worked on this farm which was managed by a Swiss company with German, Palestinian, Jordanian, and one non-Bedouin Saudi as technical advisors and administrators. The laborers, who were always spoken of as "future, potential settlers," received monthly salaries that ranged between 300 and 500 Saudi riyals ($66 to $111) while their Bedouin foreman received approximately 1000 Saudi riyals ($222). The Palestinian and Jordanian supervisors made several times this amount, with the European employees making many times as much.

These Āl Murrah laborers were joined by another group of varying size (but seldom more than twenty or twenty-five) that worked at lower paying, less prestigious jobs as *kuliya* for a German firm that was under contract to the government to drill the wells and build irrigation canals, pipelines, roads and other technical developments. This group of laborers were not expected to become settlers.

Both groups of Āl Murrah laborers lived six and eight together in bare, concrete-floored and walled rooms approximately twenty feet by ten feet, with only the barest minimum of "conveniences," none of them modern. Arranged barracks-style in long rows, these members of famous Āl Murrah lineages were joined by the vast majority of laborers at the project, most of whom came from the lower class sedentary folk from al-Hasa, Oman, the Yemen, or the Hadhramaut. Some of the Āl Murrah occasionally escaped these living quarters to stay in the tents of their relatives as these passed near Haradh or stopped for a while in the area during the course of their yearly migrations. At night the Āl Murrah tribesmen customarily forgot their work and sat around coffee fires to talk of the desert, of the rains, and of the tribe in general. At their fires they were often blessed by the arrival of a guest from their tribe. When I sat with them, they always invited me to share in their meals, begging my forgiveness that their hospitality at this camp could not be as generous as in their tents in the desert.

Aside from the unskilled laborers, two Āl Murrah families established themselves in somewhat privileged positions. One man worked as a labor contractor and was often joined by his relatives who acted as a kind of lobby with the companies and the government. One of the companies built a special concrete, Western-style house for the labor contractor and regaled him and other members of his minimal lineage with what the Germans and Swiss called *backsheesh*, particularly in the form of sheep, agricultural products such as alfalfa from the farm, and other favors as well. The other family, from the same clan, the Āl

Ghurfran, had one son working as foreman on the farm and another one working as a highly paid shop mechanic. This family also received *backsheesh*. More important, however, and to the considerable irritation of all the other Āl Murrah, the company employees habitually referred to these men as "shaikh so-and-so" and thought of them as shaikhs of the Āl Murrah. Neither family, however, was of shaikhly status within the Āl Murrah and it was, at best, derisive that they allowed themselves to be so addressed. That they did lessened their own respect within the tribe as a whole (except among their own clan) and made members of other clans extremely reluctant to seek employment at the site or to become associated with the project in any way.

No members of the actual shaikhly families of the Āl Murrah have ever had more than fleeting acquaintance with the project. Most of them were contemptuous of the way in which it was being run by the foreign contractors and of the low status that the Āl Murrah tribesmen had to take in this project, which had been announced to improve the nomads' way of life. One son of an Āl Murrah shaikh, when told confidently by a project official that the water supply was certain to be adequate for 100 years, reflected that large-scale settlement at this place would be a very unwise gamble for his tribe—after all, they have managed sufficiently well on their own for several thousand years.

Spontaneous settlement

The Āl Murrah were unique in traditional Arabia as the only major tribe which did not have some members who were permanently settled in oases. All of the other tribes traditionally had relatively large proportions (sometimes over 50 percent) of their total population in permanent settlements that played an important economic role in the life of the nomadic elements of the tribe. These settlements were the scenes of summer camps and, in most cases, individual nomads owned date palms in the oases which were cared for by the sedentary population. In return, the nomads often pastured and took care of animals that belonged to the settled folk. This pattern of symbiosis between nomadic pastoralists and settled farmers has never been studied in Arabia, but my impression is that it is, or was, the typical way in which most exchanges between nomads and settled people took place.

Because of the lack of water resources, the Āl Murrah have

never developed any permanently settled agricultural oases in
their territory. They do practice agriculture, in the form of date
palms, at four different sites—Jabrin, al-Khinn, an-Nibak, and
as-Sikak—but none of these are permanently settled. All of these
places have witnessed attempts at settlement in the past and all
of them are the scenes of contemporary activities that may lead
to the settlement of at least some of the Āl Murrah. Because they
reflect the ways in which many of the Arabian Bedouin have
traditionally attempted to integrate agriculture into their economy, it is important that we consider briefly at least one of these
oases.

Jabrin, the largest of the Āl Murrah's four oases, consists of
clumps of palm trees spread out over an area about fifteen miles
long and two to three miles wide. During the summer it is almost
exclusively inhabited by members of the Āl Jaber clan, although
all of the Āl Murrah have the right to claim unused land there
and to plant trees. The oasis is divided into localized areas, each
one of which is occupied by a different lineage of the Āl Jaber.
The amir of the Āl Jaber, ibn Muradhaf, from one of the four
shaikhly families of the Āl Murrah, makes his headquarters in the
oasis, although he camps on the outskirts of the oasis during the
fall, winter, and spring while most of the Āl Jaber are migrating.
The oasis itself is only inhabited during the summer months,
especially at the time of the date harvest in July and August.

The dates that are produced in Jabrin are considered to be of
very good quality and are much valued by the Āl Murrah and
others, especially at harvest time. They do not keep well, however, and most of them are consumed during the summer and
early fall. The trees are in a sad state of neglect which reflects the
Āl Murrah's attitudes towards agriculture. They are happy to
have this resource, but they are not much interested in actively
working at it. About the only work they do in Jabrin is to climb
the trees to collect the dates. Otherwise, the trees are left alone.
Underground water is close to the surface of the ground in
Jabrin, so irrigation is not required.

None of the Āl Murrah oases figure prominently in their
economy and contribute only marginally to their subsistence.
The herding of animals remains their major source of subsistence
and the products of the oases are consumed more as luxuries
than as staples. Socially, however, each oasis plays an important

role in the maintenance of tribal solidarity at present. Since the advent of wage labor following the development of the oil industry, many of the Āl Jaber and those who claim the other oases have begun to invest some of their cash income in the construction of summer homes in the oases. These buildings, constructed of mud-brick or of palm fronds, are inhabited by the nomads during the hot summer months. Those who are engaged in full-time wage labor return during summer vacations to the oases where they have a chance to renew their relationships with the rest of their lineage and clan. Some people are beginning to talk of modernizing the oases and of developing other types of agriculture, but so far little has been done. Schools have recently been established at all but one of the oases.

Other spontaneous attempts at settlement reflect the large-scale economic changes that are taking place. Increasing numbers of the Āl Murrah are abandoning pastoralism altogether and working for wages. Their herds are either sold or entrusted to the care of relatives. This process began in the 1950s and is increasing at present. Many tribespeople have settled in shanty town complexes built of scrap materials. At least three such shanty towns belong to or are predminantly inhabited by members of the Āl Murrah. Although some of them have developed some agriculture, all of them have settled because of their activities in industrial occupations.

One of these shanty towns is located just off the Riyadh-Dhahran highway about five miles west of Abquaiq. It is composed of over thirty housing units each one of which typically has an enclosed, subdivided yard and two or three rooms with separate nonconnecting entrances. One room is a *majlis,* or men's sitting room, while the other rooms are reserved for women. All of the structures, including the wall encircling the yard, are made of tin and scrap lumber, much of which has been scavenged from oil company buildings no longer in use which have been torn down. Each year, most of these edifices see improvements, such as concrete floors and plywood walls inside the rooms.

About two-thirds of the residents of this shanty town are from the Āl Murrah, the others being mainly from the Beni Hajir tribe. Among the Āl Murrah contingent are groups of households which are closely related genealogically, but this new town does not conform to any of the principles of lineage and clan social organization. This settlement, then, is not itself a unit in the tribal social structure, as is Jabrin, and the people who live there do not think of themselves as a special community set off against the rest of the world. Each household just happens to be there while the other members of their social community are herding camels in the desert. Needless to say, some kind of social life does take place within this community, but there is no village or town organization and a man looks to his nomadic tribal leader as his leader and would plan to intermarry with his nomadic kinspeople rather than with other families in his settlement.

All of the people resident in this settlement either work or have worked for the oil company at Abquaiq or are or have been in the service of ibn Jiluwi, the amir of al-Hasa, or some other government agency. None of them are newcomers to the urban environment but started work for ARAMCO or for the government at least twenty years ago. Some of them, at this settlement and at others like it, have participated in ARAMCO schemes that led to the building of villas in places like Hofuf and Abquaiq, but many of these have been abandoned, partially abandoned or rented out to other people, their owners preferring to live outside the cities.

Even if one does not live with his own tribal kin, by living outside the town or the city he can at least convive with other fellow ex-nomads and avoid continuous interaction with the traditionally sedentary populations. With more room to expand, many carry on some sheep and goat herding acitivities, grazing their animals in the outskirts of the settlement. Agricultural gardens, with date palms and plants such as tomatoes and particularly alfalfa, have been developed. In all instances, however, the agricultural gardens are worked by hired laborers, while their owners work for ARAMCO or at other high-paying jobs in the town. The owner's sons often commute, along with their fathers, to the nearby town where they study. Whatever pastoral activities they maintain are done by the women. About half these households keep tents, and their families, especially the women and younger sons, move out to graze their sheep and goats in the desert during part of the winter and spring. During summer vacation, most of the young sons and many of the women enjoy a visit with their camel-owning relatives at their wells deep in the desert. In all instances, these people have either sold or entrusted any camels they may have owned to their nomadic kin.

ĀL MURRAH ATTITUDES TOWARDS SETTLEMENT

The Āl Murrah do not look down on sedentarization per se, in spite of the fact that they hold most sedentary people in Saudi Arabia in low esteem. All of them are consciously aware of the present-day trend of many Saudi Arabian nomads to settle—at least partially. Most of them recognize that benefits can accrue from some aspects of settlement, and they desire to have some kind of participation in this general process. Few of them, however, want to abandon their camels and give up pastoralism altogether, and almost everyone would ideally like to have at least a summer house and a small agricultural plot with some date palms. If the agricultural plot should require the full-time employment of a family member and produce a return worthy of his full-time employment, then every *bayt* would be willing and able to spare a member for such an activity; but none of them want to abandon the tent and the herd in an abrupt change to settled life for the whole group. While sentimentality certainly plays a part in not wanting to abandon pastoralism, practicality is without doubt the major conscious reason.

During the summer of 1969, a number of leading men from the Āl Jaber clan at Jabrin spoke against the nomads abandoning their tried and sure way of life. One of them reasoned that the whole Arabian Peninsula is a sparse land and that, while the nomads and the sedentary peasants have always managed to live off their animals and their dates, the large number of recent immigrants into Saudi Arabia can only be fed by buying rice and other foods with money from the oil industry. "The oil wells," he said, "can be blown up in thirty minutes and, with no money, all those people in Dhahran and Riyadh would die from lack of food. Why, they would not even have enough gasoline to leave and go back to their homelands."

The nomads are keenly aware of the delicate ecological balance that exists in most of Arabia, and while some drought years are difficult, they all have a sense of their long history of survival and of their pre-eminence as a powerful tribe since primeval days, long before the beginning of Islam. They are rightly suspicious of the available water resources and are highly reluctant to shift their dependence to nonproven, well-irrigated agriculture. Sedentarization in conjunction with nonagricultural activities, such as industrial or commercial activities, is seldom mentioned, although most of the nomads who have settled in Saudi Arabia have done so because of their involvement with the oil companies or their work as drivers or in governmental service.

When survival is not in question, sedentarization is acceptable to the Āl Murrah so long as certain social criteria are maintained. Most of the Āl Jaber leaders, for example, opposed the idea of Jabrin being modernized and developed on any kind of scale similar to that of the King Faisal Settlement Project at Haradh sixty kilometers to the north. They felt this would bring in large numbers of unwanted foreigners and many nontribal Saudi Arabians. As a result, Jabrin would cease to be a tribal gathering place where both nomads and their sedentarized relatives could interact together as a brotherhood, where they could be together in their own world. Other Āl Murrah echo this feeling of the Āl Jaber for tribal isolation when they say that settlement is acceptable so long as one's people, particularly the lineage, stays together. The spontaneous shanty town settlements outside the major cities are looked down on by most nomads because this essentially represents a man's break from his tribal grouping. A lineage settlement, however, located at a convenient place in one's territory, inhabited either full-time or part-time by some of the lineage members and visited at least occasionally by nomads from one's own lineage, is not only acceptable but ideal. Improvement projects in the existing oases or new developments might well include training programs for the young Āl Murrah who are currently going off to work in semi-technical jobs in the oil industry. Programs that would allow them to stay at home and do much of the improvement and development work themselves would result in a much higher degree of success than is possible by importing foreign technical experts who know nothing of the language, culture, or society.

In preferring lineage settlements, the Āl Murrah acknowledge the basic importance of the lineage as a unit in their social organization. They might also approve of closely related lineages from a clan sharing a settlement, but the mixture of clans in any kind of settlement is considered a difficult business, since each clan is expected to look out for its own aggrandizement and one's loyalty beyond clan lines often wears thin. Political leadership is centered around the clan groupings, and the relative displacement of one clan by another in the economy or politics of any settlement would surely lead to "unhealthy, non-tribal" competition. Furthermore, since the present spatial organization of the clans results in their dispersal over a large territory, the combination of clans in any single place would mean the removal of all but one from its own major traditional grazing lands.

A notion of politics, also, plays a role in the Āl Murrah's attitudes towards settlement. Aside from economic and ecological problems and general lack of administrative direction, one of the major barriers to the successful development of the King Faisal Settlement Project is due to its grand scale. Some of the lineages and clans which exploit the outlying area of the site are loathe to participate in it, even as laborers, because of the predominating influence of the Āl Ghurfran clan and some of their leading figures in the project. From another point of view, some of the traditional leading men of the tribe fear full-time settlement as a means of facilitating political subservience of the tribe to the nation-state. Nomads, they reason, are not so easily coerced for political purposes if they migrate and are not tied to any specific piece of land. Isolated villages, as a result, are preferred to others close to town, since there will be less encouragement for mixing with non-tribal elements and since the greater one's isolation, the greater one's freedom.

The Āl Murrah do not identify themselves exclusively as herders or nomads. Their strongest identification is a social one, that of tribespeople. If they can maintain their tribal way of life, they have no major objections to settlement. But whether they can maintain their segmentary tribal organization is doubtful. Their social organization, as we have shown in earlier chapters, is part of their adaptation as nomadic pastoralists. Settlement implies greater concentrations of people and a kind of rigidity that prohibits the process of fission and fusion. Their recent settlement in shanty towns already reflects a *de facto* break in the tribal social organization, although most of the settlers continue to think of themselves as members of the tribe. We can expect the tribal organization to maintain itself at least partially only if settlement is planned on a large-scale throughout Arabia and if conscious attempts are made to decentralize these settlements in such a way that small groups of kin can settle together and combine pastoralism with other activities. Whether this will occur is doubtful, but what the Āl Murrah would like is to be actively incorporated into both the planning and the implementation of projects destined to change their way of life, even in small degrees. Without their incorporation in every stage of development, any projects designed to help them can only hope to be marginally successful at best.

CHANGES IN NOMADIC PASTORALISM

Perhaps the most interesting but least discussed change that has occurred in rural Saudi Arabia is the change the Bedouin are making from herding camels for subsistence to herding sheep and goats for subsistence and for sale in the urban markets. Most commentators on contemporary Saudi Arabia state that the Bedouin have all but ceased to exist and believe that they have abandoned the desert and settled in urban communities. Many urban Saudi Arabians share this belief, which is based on the undeniable fact that many Bedouin *have* settled in and around the cities and that those who remain in the desert have become almost invisible. They are invisible to the townspeople because they dress much the same as other people in Saudi Arabia today—especially the men—and because they no longer ride into town on camels but rather in shiny new pickup trucks. My guess, however, is that there are just as many herds and tents operating in the deserts of Arabia today as there were before the rise of the oil industry. Such is the case among the Āl Murrah, and from what they say, this holds true for other tribes as well.

Individual members of Bedouin families have settled and have established households in towns, but as we saw in chapter three, most traditional Bedouin households included more than one nuclear family. In most cases there were more people than were actually needed to do the work connected with herding, so each herd supported more people than it required. Thus it has been relatively easy for many Bedouin families to divide in such a way that some of their members go to work in the urban environment while others continue to keep herds in the desert. This occurs today among the most traditional camel herders like the Āl 'Azab, but it is especially true of the majority of Saudi Arabian Bedouin who have switched from herding camels to herding sheep and goats.

The change from camels to sheep and goats is directly dependent on the development of underground water resources through the drilling of deep wells operated by mechanical pumps and the use of trucks in connection with herding. Both of these factors have greatly increased the potential for sheep and goat herding in the interior of the desert. Previously, the camel was the only animal that could be taken to many of the better grazing areas of the desert because of the lack of water resources. Sheep and goats do not have the same ability to forgo water for long periods of time that camels have and, as a result, the herding of these animals has been restricted to areas close to water resources. The development of deep wells has opened up large areas of the desert that were once used only by camels to sheep and goats. The use of trucks has also contributed to this change, since the Bedouin are now able to truck water directly to the herds without having to take them to the wells. They can also move the sheep and goats by truck directly to the grazing areas. Many of the well sites have witnessed the development of small service towns whose populations include semisedentary pastoralists, merchants, police, teachers, and, in many cases, a few farmers, since the development of agriculture is sometimes an important part of these new settlements. The development of these new towns has also contributed to the invisibility of the pastoralists in the larger cities, since many of the services once obtainable only in the city are now extended into the hinterland and the Bedouin who continue to herd have less need to go to the city.

While these changes have been occurring in the desert, the Saudi Arabian urban population has been increasing rapidly—both in absolute size and in purchasing power. The demand for meat products and other foods has accordingly sky-rocketed in Saudi Arabia. Much of this increased demand has been met through the importation of huge quantities of food from abroad. Frozen mutton is shipped in from New Zealand, Australia, and Argentina, and herds of camels are shipped in from Sudan. The desert hinterland of Saudi Arabia has also begun to supply this increased urban demand, although by no means to the extent that it is capable.

In Saudi Arabia, mutton is the preferred meat of the urban population. Camel meat, much prized by the Bedouin, is the meat of the urban poor, since most of the camel meat sold there comes from the slaughter of old camels and is very tough. The Bedouin also think of camels as milk animals and, in the past, as transport animals, and have never raised them primarily for meat. Although one scholar, Richard Bulliet (personal communication), argues that camels are a potentially important meat animal in desert areas, since they eat thorn and other plants for which other animals seldom compete, I know of no studies of the comparative advantages of sheep versus camels as meat producers in desert areas. At any rate, a large proportion of Saudi Arabian Bedouin have, in the last two decades, switched from herding camels to herding sheep and goats. The sheep are potentially destined for urban consumption, while the goats provide milk and milk products for the herders.

The change from camels to sheep and goats has been spontaneous among the Bedouin and not the result of any governmental or other outside encouragement. Because of the very nature of their acculturation as pastoralists, it is not surprising that the Bedouin have automatically responded to changing conditions in Saudi Arabia by introducing changes themselves in the area of activity they not only know best but regard as their special domain. They love animals and know a great deal about them. On the other hand, they despise agriculture and know almost nothing about it. As nomads, they are highly conditioned to operating independently for long periods of time in the desert, and during the thousands of years of their adaptation, they have come to value their independence. To become wholly sedentarized and to live in a compact settlement with nonkinspeople is anathema to most of the Bedouin.

Contact between the Bedouin and the sedentary people in Arabia is not new. As we have shown, the Bedouin tribes do not form social and economic islands in Arabia but have traditionally been part of a wider economic and social system, although exchange between the Bedouin and the sedentary people has usually been limited. As modernization occurs in Saudi Arabia, both the Bedouin and the sedentary people are equally open to change. Because of their past ecological adaptation, the Bedouin not only possess skills as herders but have evolved a type of social organization, that of segmentary tribal groups, that fits well with their herding practices. They have their own subculture which both reflects and reinforces their specialized herding activities.

Consequently, to force them to abandon herding—as some governments have wanted—would necessitate major social and cultural changes and at the same time result in the complete loss of the area the pastoralists have traditionally exploited. In Saudi Arabia, where animal protein is in increasingly great demand and where the desert hinterland has the capability of supplying an important part of this demand, it would obviously be unfortunate not to continue to exploit this resource. What kinds of specific changes have the Bedouin themselves initiated?

Before the development of modern wells in the desert, sheep and goat herding was the exclusive concern of lower status tribes who were often politically subservient to the major camel herding tribes who militarily protected them. The opposite is true nowadays, since the richest and most influential nomads are those who have large herds of sheep. This includes a majority of the major tribes of camel nomads with the sole exception of the Āl Murrah in Saudi Arabia. The Āl Murrah have changed less than the other tribes because of their territory: the Rub' al-Khali is not conducive to sheep herding because of the long distances which separate areas of sparse vegetation. Most of the Āl Murrah, however, who have a foot hold outside the Rub' al-Khali have changed or are in the process of changing to sheep and goats. The sheep and goat herds of the Āl Murrah are on a whole smaller than those of the other tribes who made the change earlier, but their new experiences are all similar.

In comparison with camels, sheep and goats demand much less attention from the herders. Camels range over great expanses of territory, with herds divided into three or four subunits. Each herd of camels requires at least two full-time herders and one part-time herder. One herder, however, can manage a large flock of sheep and goats grazing, while more help is needed in milking a large flock and in obtaining water for them. Sheep and goat herding is a more sedentary activity. Like their camel herding counterparts, sheep and goat herders spend the summer months camped at permanent sources of water, and migrate during the other seasons to wherever rains have created pasturage, yet they seldom move more than five or six times a year. The Āl 'Azab camel nomads move at least sixty times during the fall, winter, and spring.

The change from camels to sheep and goats causes different work patterns for both men and women, allowing more freedom to pursue a variety of activities not directly related to herding. Because they can spend less time moving, sheep and goat herding women can produce more household goods; the Āl 'Azab women in the camel herding groups I knew were so busy moving they had little time for any other production. They knew how to weave, but they seldom worked at it and produced only the items needed for their immediate household, never any for sale. The women of sheep and goat herding groups, however, are beginning to find lucrative outlets for Bedouin rugs, saddle bags, and other decorative items. These women, who have more time to prepare food, make several varieties of goat's cheese and ghee from animal fat. By far the best cooks in the desert, they serve a great variety of well-prepared food. Camel nomad women, on the other hand, with less than an hour a day for food preparation, neither process camel's milk nor regularly prepare any elaborate meals.

The women of sheep and goat herding units take an active role in managing the herds. Indeed, the women are often exclusively in charge of both the household and the herd, while the men are away working for wages, studying, or serving in the military. Among the camel herders, both the men and the women are always present. Increasingly, the Saudi Arabian Bedouin hire other Bedouin from impoverished areas in Iraq, Jordan, and Syria to herd their sheep and goats while they work in urban areas and only occasionally visit their herds and families. As a result, a kind of nomadic ranching complex may be emerging in the deserts of Saudi Arabia. Although the herds must still move to different grazing areas for different seasons, it is no longer necessary for the family to base their subsistence exclusively on herding. They can combine herding with other activities and thus achieve a higher standard of living within the modern economy. Since there is a high urban demand for their products, the pastoralists can make important contributions to the national economy.

It is too early to judge how successful the Bedouin will ultimately be in switching from subsistence-oriented camel herding to market-oriented herding of sheep and goats. Some fear ecological disaster may ensue since sheep and goats graze more thoroughly than do camels; overgrazing has already occurred in some areas. But this problem could easily be controlled through active programs of range management, something the Bedouin already understand in principle and have demonstrated in their restricted grazing of different areas under traditional patterns of herding.

What they really need is the active encouragement and cooperation of the government. Already the government has contributed significantly through the development and maintenance of wells, through helping the Bedouin obtain trucks, and through the building of new towns. But the Bedouin need better marketing facilities to encourage them to get their animals in from the desert and into the cities at the right time. Modern feed lots would help to fatten animals before they are slaughtered for consumption by the urban people. There are indications that the government is beginning to act according to these needs. Indeed, the Haradh project is now being developed as a way station to fatten sheep for the urban market rather than as a large-scale Bedouin agricultural settlement. There are still many problems—not the least of which is the continuation of many of the old cultural prejudices that have traditionally existed between the nomads and the sedentary folk in the Middle East.

It is my hope, however, that the changes the Bedouin have spontaneously initiated in their own pastoral activities will merit the close scrutiny of both scientists and government officials. The Bedouin, who prefer their camels—by far more fascinating and more lovable beasts than sheep and goats—also know the capacity of the desert. Now that the herding of sheep and goats appears to accommodate the demands of the modernized urban society, they are willing and eager to accommodate themselves accordingly. As we have seen throughout this book, the Bedouin are very practical in their life style, and they do not now want to lose the desert environment that has produced so successfully for them throughout many thousands of years. We, too, in our overcrowded world beset with declining ratios of food to people can little afford to lose that environment either. Thus, as any of the Bedouin would readily point out, it is not romanticism but practicality that demands the continuation of nomadic pastoralism in the modern world.

Bibliography

Barth, Fredrik
  1961 *Nomads of South Persia: The Basseri Tribe of the Khamseh Confederacy.* Oslo: University of Oslo Publications.

Bujra, Abdalla S.
  1971 *The Politics of Stratification: A Study of Political Change in a South Arabian Town.* Oxford: Oxford University Press.

Cressey, George B.
  1960 *Crossroads: Land and Life in Southwest Asia.* Chicago: Lippincott.

Dickson, H. R. P.
  1949 *The Arab of the Desert: A Glimpse into Badawin Life in Kuwait and Saudi Arabia.* London: Murray.

Evans-Pritchard, Sir Edward E.
  1940 *The Nuer: A Description of the Modes of Livelihood and Political Institutions of a Nilotic People.* Oxford: Oxford University Press.

  1949 *The Sanusi of Cyrenaica.* Oxford: Oxford University Press.

Fathy, Hassan
  1969 *Gourna: A Tale of Two Villages.* Cairo: Ministry of Culture Publications.

Fernea, Robert A.
1970 *Shaykh and Effendi: Changing Patterns of Authority Among the El Shabana of Southern Iraq.* Cambridge: Harvard University Press.

Ibn Khaldun
1958 *The Muqaddimah: An Introduction to History.* Translated from the Arabic by Franz Rosenthal. New York: Pantheon Books.

Lattimore, Owen
1962 *Nomads and Commissars: Mongolia Revisited.* New York: Oxford University Press.

Musil, Alois
1927 *Arabia Deserta: A Topographical Itinerary.* New York: American Geographical Society.

Peters, Emrys
1960 "The Proliferation of Segments in the Lineage of the Bedouin of Cyrenaica." *Journal of the Royal Anthropological Institute* 90:29–53.

1968 "The Tied and the Free." In J. G. Peristiany, ed., *Contributions to Mediterranean Sociology: Mediterranean Rural Communities and Social Change.* Athens: Publications of the Social Science Center.

Polk, William R.
1973 *Passing Brave.* New York: Knopf.

Rahman, Fazlur
1968 *Islam.* New York: Doubleday.

Salim, S. M.
1962 *The Marsh Dwellers of the Euphrates Delta.* London: Athlone.

Smithers, R.
1966 *The Haradh Project.* Beirut: The Ford Foundation. MS.

Sweet, Louise E.
1965 "Camel Raiding of North Arabian Bedouin: A Mechanism of Ecological Adaptation." *American Anthropologist* 67: 1132–1150.

Thesiger, Wilfred
    1959 *Arabian Sands*. London: Longmans.

Uhlig, Dieter
    n.d. "King Faisal Settlement Project Haradh/Saudi Arabia."
    WAKUTI Consulting Company.

Wolf, Eric R.
    1951 "The Social Organization of Mecca and the Origins of
    Islam." *Southwestern Journal of Anthropology* 7:329–356.

Suggested Further Reading

Asad, Talal

    1970 *The Kababish Arabs: Power, Authority, and Consent in a Nomadic Tribe*. London: C. Hurst and Company.

        An excellent account of the political structure of a large tribe of camel nomads in Sudan, this book provides a description of the ecological framework within which this tribe operates and analyses the social and economic conditions that allow a small elite to dominate the tribe as a whole.

Barth, Fredrik

    1961 *Nomads of South Persia: The Basseri Tribe of the Khamseh Confederacy*. Boston: Little, Brown and Company.

        One of the first modern anthropological monographs on Middle Eastern nomads, this book takes an explicit ecological perspective and presents a careful analysis of the relationship between the environment and the segmentary social organization of the tribe. The book also discusses the political, economic, and demographic processes that serve to maintain the tribe as a persisting unit in relation to the outside.

Bujra, Abdalla S.

    1971 *The Politics of Stratification: A Study of Political Change in a South Arabian Town*. Oxford: Oxford University Press.

        This book describes the complex structure of traditional society in South Arabia. While it focuses on the sedentary population, it clearly shows the ways in which nomadic tribes fit into Arabian politics and economics, especially before the advent of centralized national authority structures.

Dickson, H. R. P.
1951 *The Arab of the Desert: A Glimpse into Badawin Life in Kuwait and Sau'di Arabia.* London: Allen and Unwin.
A classic account of Bedouin life in eastern Arabia by a British political agent, this book contains many, personal anecdotes and attempts a kind of encyclopedic listing of the major features of Bedouin culture.

Doughty, Charles
1936 *Travels in Arabia Deserta.* London: Johnathan Cape.
Perhaps the greatest travel book ever, this classic is based on the author's experiences wandering in northern Arabia during the latter part of the 19th century. It provides a multitude of intimate accounts of nomadic and sedentary life in pre-modern Arabia.

Evans-Pritchard, Sir Edward E.
1949 *The Sanusi of Cyrenaica.* Oxford: Oxford University Press.
An important work by a leading social anthropologist, this book concisely describes the ecology of nomadism in eastern Libya and the segmentary social organization of the tribes there, all within the context of an historical study of the structure of the Sanusi religio-political movement which bears many parallels with the Wahabi movement in Arabia.

Musil, Alois
1928 *The Manners and Customs of the Rwala Bedouins.* New York: American Geographical Society.
A famous study of one of the largest and most powerful Bedouin tribes located mainly in Jordan and Syria, this monograph provides a wealth of material on Bedouin folk-lore, as well as a good description of the ecological frame-work. It records many poems and sayings of the Rwala.

Nelson, Cynthia, ed.
1973 *The Desert and the Sown: Nomads in the Wider Society.* Berkeley: University of California, Institute of International Studies.
This book is a collection of papers presented at a symposium devoted to studying the ways in which nomadic tribes, especially in the Middle East, relate to the wider society in which they live. All of the papers are by anthropologists who have recently done fieldwork among nomads in the area.

Philby, H. St. John
1933 *The Empty Quarter.* New York: Henry Holt and Company.

Although this book contains numerous minor errors, especially concerning the Āl Murrah, it provides a vast amount of geographical information about the Rub' al-Khali by the second Westerner to ever travel there.

Rentz, George

1972 "Wahhabism and Saudi Arabia". In Derek Hopwood, ed., *The Arabian Peninsula: Society and Politics*. London: George Allen and Unwin.

This article provides a useful history of the Wahabi movement and the creation of the modern state of Saudi Arabia.

Thesiger, Wilfred

1959 *Arabian Sands*. London: Longmans.

This is a beautifully written and sensitive portrayal of the desolate beauty of the Rub' al-Khali, the rigors of living there, and the skills of the Bedouin who consider it home. The author traveled throughout the region by camel for four years during the 1940's and has given us an intimate description of the area and especially of the character and personalities of the young Bedouin among whom he lived and traveled.

Glossary

Abal. The name of a bush which grows in the Rub' al-Khali and which provides the main source of pasturage for camels in that region.

Agid. Commander of a raiding party; a title of respect given to famous Bedouin warriors.

'Ain. Well; eye.

Al-asferi. Autumn.

Al-gaidh. Summer camp.

Al-ghazzu. Raid.

Al-harb. War; warfare.

Amir. Literally, a commander. A title given to princes and tribal leaders or chiefs in Saudi Arabia.

'Arabna. Our Arabs—often used by Āl Murrah Bedouin to refer to the women of their households.

'Arifa. Sage; wise old man who arbitrated Bedouin disputes according to customary tribal law before governmental centralization of legal processes.

Ar-rabi'ah. The name of a short season that occurs only during years of very good rainfall when grasses and bushes are especially luxuriant. It lasts from four to eight weeks during the latter part of the winter.

Ar-rub' al-khali. The Empty Quarter.

Ash-shita. Winter.

Ash-Shuruf. The name of a very fine breed of milk camels which are black in color.

As-seif. Spring, among the Bedouin; summer, among the sedentary people.

Ayal al-batn. Children of the womb—refers to people related to each other through the mother but with different fathers.

Ayal 'amm. Father's brother's children or descendants.

'Aynin. Tribal leaders.

Az-ziman al-aishb. The season of the winter grasses.

Banat al-hawa. Literally daughters of the wind; "loose" women.

Bayt. Tent; household.

Bint 'amm. A man's father's brother's daughter, the preferred woman for a man to marry.

Bir. Well.

Clan. A unit of social organization which groups together several lineages as the common descendants of an ancestor.

Dar. Homestead. It includes the tent and the area around it. Several households which camp together occupy a single *dar*.

Dirat-Āl Murrah. Āl Murrah territories.

Diya. Blood money; indemnity.

Dowla. The state.

'Erg. Sand dune.

Fakhd. Lineage. Literally, thigh.

Gabila. Tribe; clan.

Gadi. Religious judge.

Gasir. Neighbor. Refers to the relationship between members of different households in a *dar*.

Gasr. Palace; permanent, traditional-style house.

Galamat. Artesian well.

Goz. Sand hill.

Hadith. Traditions; especially the acts and sayings of the Prophet Muhammad which, along with the Koran, are a major source of Islamic law.

Haji. Pilgrim.

Hakim. Ruler; judge.

Helal. Righteous; virtuous.

Hema. Wall of a tent.

Hujra (sg.) *hujar* (pl.). Room; house; settlement—especially an Ikhwan settlement.

Hukuma. Literally, the rulers; the government.

Ibn 'ammi. Son of my father's brother.

Ikhwan. Brothers; brotherhood.

Imam. Muslim religious leader.

Inshallah. If God wills.

Jazirah. Island.

Jihad. Holy War.

Jinn (masc.), *Jinnia* (fem.). Spirits; genies.

Kohl. Black cosmetic used as an eye-liner.

Lineage. A unit of social organization which groups together all the descendants of an ancestor who, in the case of the Āl Murrah, lived about five generations ago. The lineage is subdivided into *minimal lineages* which group together all the descendants of an ancestor who lived two to three generations ago. The *maximal lineage* refers to the full lineage grouping.

Maktub. Literally, written—in the sense of preordained; predestined.

Malik. King.

Majlis. Sitting room; reception hall; court; audience.

Mujahidin. Holy Warriors.

Ru'ag. Tapestry-like divider woven by the women to separate the men's and women's sections of a tent.

Sharif. Noble.

Shari'a. Islamic Law.

Shetan. Devils.

Suq. Market; bazaar.

'Ulama'. Religious leaders.

Umara'. Political leaders; princes.

Umtowa. Religious specialist.

Wadi. Valley; dry river basin.

Wasta. Go-between.

Wasm. Brand.

Ydhakil. Literally, he goes in. Refers to the consummation of a marriage, when the man goes in to his bride in a special part of the tent that has been prepared for them.

Zakat. Religious tax.

Index